The Two-Minute Tune-Up

Daily Inspirational Messages

Pam Boyd

For the *Emotional Dominance* You Need
Every Day of Your Valuable Life!

iUniverse, Inc.
Bloomington

The Two-Minute Tune-Up
Daily Inspirational Messages

Interior photographs and all poems or quotes that are not cited are original.

iUniverse books may be ordered through booksellers or by contacting:

iUniverse
1663 Liberty Drive
Bloomington, IN 47403
www.iuniverse.com
1-800-Authors (1-800-288-4677)

ISBN: 978-1-4697-9814-1 (sc)
ISBN: 978-1-4697-9815-8 (hc)
ISBN: 978-1-4697-9816-5 (e)

Library of Congress Control Number: 2012904938

Printed in the United States of America

iUniverse rev. date: 3/20/2012

For Jan, who has always given me the right book at the right time, and for the many people and numerous authors who taught me the importance of a daily tune-up early in life.

An unexamined life is not worth living.
—Socrates

Introduction

How long does it take for someone to ruin your day? Not long; probably two minutes or less. You've probably experienced that phenomenon many times; you were feeling just great until some insensitive person or thoughtless act totally turned your mood around—*snap!* Just like that.

Fortunately, it only takes two minutes or less for us to turn our own moods around as well. Simply by taking two minutes at the start of each day to focus outside of the small, narrow construct of our own worlds, we can be completely refreshed—and, ultimately, tap into our own *emotional dominance. Snap!*

Instead of getting out of bed and *hoping* that today will be good, *we can choose the day we want to have.* We may not be able to control certain events or other people, but we can always control our emotional responses to the people and things in our lives. Our days *never* have to be an experiment, a wager, a mystery, a chance, or a disappointment. We never have to be at the mercy of someone or something else. If we have emotional dominance, we have the power to decide what our day is *before it happens.* As easily as we turn the channel on our television sets, we can *decide* which "movie" we want to play in our own lives, simply by seizing control of our thoughts.

Taking time for a *Two-Minute Tune-Up* every day is really about taking back the remote control for our own lives from whomever or whatever we have handed it to. And the transfer of power takes only a few minutes a day!

Look at it like this: can you imagine starting your day without washing your face, brushing your teeth, or taking a shower? *No!* We're smart enough to know that these rituals not only make us feel better but also make us far more pleasant to be around. *The same goes for our minds.* Our minds need to be cleaned and refreshed just as much as our bodies do—particularly because our emotions spring from our thoughts.

Can you imagine discovering that your car has a dead battery, ignoring it, and pretending you can drive to work as usual? *No!* You are smart enough to know that the only way to get your car going is to find someone with a live battery who can give the car a good *jump-start.* You must borrow power from another source. It's a very logical process. But, as ridiculous as it seems, some of us expect our lives to run, even though we never charge our mental batteries. No wonder we're depressed and sluggish when the coffee or energy-drink wears off. It's no wonder some of us never find the motivation to get off the couch.

Even more ridiculous: Can you imagine driving your car with four flat tires? Can you imagine expecting your car to run forever without changing the oil or giving it a tune-up? *No!* We know better than that. But we have forgotten that our minds need tune-ups as much as our cars do.

The reasons we have forgotten are not that complicated. We are busy. We have obligations. We are too tired to get up even two minutes earlier. I can relate.

I made a commitment during my first year of university to have a quiet time every morning, but too often "more important things" took over the time slot or I sat through the meditation like a zombie, with a mind too distracted to concentrate. Over the years, I have improved and am so grateful that I never gave up this practice.

I used to tell people that I was going to have a T-shirt printed saying, *After working on my character for thirty-something years, this*

T-shirt is all I have to show for it. Sometimes life felt that way. But, in spite of all the detours, disappointments, and difficult years, I really don't believe that any time invested in personal development was wasted.

In fact, I know, without a doubt, that daily, incremental devotion to self-improvement has had a powerful cumulative effect on the person I am today. Following are some of the specific pay-offs and take-aways in my personal and professional life:

- *more power and confidence* as a public speaker (in forty-nine states and six countries)
- *more insight* as an international leadership and management consultant
- *more creativity and inspiration* as an artist (award-winning feature filmmaker, poet, author of three books and three screenplays, and visual artist)
- *more love* as a partner
- *more friendships* that are broader, richer, and stronger
- *more sensitivity* as a mother of three, step-parent of two, and trustee for my niece and special-needs nephew
- *more understanding* as the primary caregiver for my mother when she suffered from Alzheimer's
- *more incentive* for physical fitness (tennis, golf, and running)
- *more peace* dealing with death, illness, and trauma

The back story behind *The Two-Minute Tune-up* is my own need for tune-ups. I began a daily journal many years ago so that I wouldn't lose any of the lessons I was learning. Often, the insights I recorded would re-surface in conversations with friends, coworkers, and clients. Later, I began casually posting some of my epiphanies on Facebook. When my friends said it was helping them, I started a daily blog. Then, when my subscribers asked for a compilation, a book was the next step.

My hope is that *The Two-Minute Tune-Up* will serve as your daily port of renewal: a place to recharge, flip your switch from idle to full power, and realign the wheels of your life. I also hope that you will take time daily to record your reactions to the tune-up and how it applies to your own circumstances. By doing so, you will multiply the effectiveness of the reflective practice. I have left space on each page for this purpose. Your informal notations will also serve as a personal growth journal and, later, as a window into that day of your life—*a valuable gift to your future.*

Thank you for including *The Two-Minute Tune-Up* as part of the sacred journey of your *one* amazing and valuable life!

January

Beginnings

I should have no objection to go over the same life from its beginning to the end: requesting only the advantage authors have, of correcting in a second edition the faults of the first.

—*Benjamin Franklin*

January 1

"I Did It, I Admit It" Day

Today, go for the joy of the *clean slate*. Why not take care of the uncomfortable moments? You know—the ones that sneak up on you when you are thinking about something else or when you are just about to fall asleep, the ones that wake you in the middle of the night—the *why-did-I-do-that?* moments, the *I-really-should-give-that-DVD-back-to-them-but-it's-a-hassle-and-it's-been-so-long* moments, and the *I-should-apologize-but-it's-too-humiliating* moments.

We all have them. No better day to clear our consciences. I'll do it if you do it. What a difference it will make—for all of us.

January 2

New Year's Resolutions Don't Work ...

They don't work, that is, unless we love and respect ourselves. If we are beating ourselves up, swimming against the tide, focusing on the pain of it all, we've already lost. The place to start is to feel good about who we are and acknowledge that we are worthy, valuable, and honorable.

Just in case no one else has told you today: *You are worthy, valuable, and honorable—just the way you are! The world needs the real you.*

Believe it. Say it. Tape it on your mirror or your forehead. However you accomplish it, please tap into the confidence this knowledge creates—*before* you make any resolution or start any project. Otherwise, without this energy behind you, your resolution will be a *de-motivator* before February arrives.

January 3

You Have *Not* Arrived

One day, when I was in a race to the airport to catch a flight, almost everything that could go wrong did. Worry, frustration, and anger took over—*until I recognized that the airport was not my real destination*. When I decided to head toward *peace* rather than the airport, my circumstances improved radically.

All worked out. My flight had been delayed. There was never anything to stress about. *But* if I had continued to worry about getting to the airport, I would have punished myself and ultimately, everyone around me, *needlessly*.

Peace is always the real destination. If we get to where we are going *without peace,* we have *not* arrived.

January 4

Don't Worry if the Night Forgets Your Name

When I feel *anonymous*, I have turned to these words by Rilke for confidence. Even typing these stanzas empowers me. I hope it does the same for you—*because the world needs your voice!*

Silent friend of many distances, feel
How your breath enlarges space
From the dark rafters of the belfry let the peal
Of yourself ring out, each bat become a lark …
Don't worry if the night forgets your name
Affirm to the quiet earth: I flow.
Play to the crowded waters, pianissimo.

— *Rainer Maria Rilke* (Braybrooke 2001)

Whatever our circumstances, we have a voice. I hope you will use yours and begin to affirm your place with confidence—today.

January 5

How Are You Leaving People?

I have always aspired to live by Mother Teresa's admonition, "Let no one come to you without leaving better and happier." I can't say I've always done that, but reading these words helps me think more about what state I am leaving people in *in my wake*. I have to admit that sometimes I've made people *bitter* instead of *better*. Oops.

Although, I am *very* proud of the times I have had the right effect. Here's the best Mother Teresa-like compliment I ever received: "Usually, after the workshops I have to go slug down some drinks to get over it, but you made two hours go by very quickly."

I think that counts, don't you?

January 6

Sing It Like You Mean It!

I love that scene in the movie *Walk the Line* when the producer tells aspiring artist Johnny Cash that he doesn't want to hear the *same old song*—but instead the song he would sing if it were his last.

This one piece of advice changes my day more than just about anything else that I might think about. If I remember, first thing in the morning, to *sing my day like it's the last song I'll ever sing*, I bring *my entire self* with me into the day and am *fully engaged* in whatever capacity I am needed.

Then I am not only interested *and* interesting—I am *electric*.

January 7

Really Hearing

Reviewing the past year, I have to admit I am only just now learning to *really listen* to the people in my life who push my emotional buttons. I'm embarrassed to admit this because I teach the principles every week.

Last month, when my nephew called me, disgusted and complaining about his dad, instead of correcting him as I usually do with, "You shouldn't think that way or say those things," I simply said, "You seem really sad and hurt." I allowed him to express his pain, and I mirrored it back to him instead of escalating the drama with my platitudes (that he had heard a million times). Duh.

He calmed down immediately once he knew I *really* heard him.

January 8

Are You Repelling the Positive?

More Rilke:

There is only a single, urgent task: to attach oneself to that which is strong, striving, and bright with unreserved readiness, and then to move forward in one's efforts without any calculation or guile.

—*Rainer Maria Rilke* (Ulrich 2005)

Yesterday, I wasn't feeling strong, striving, or bright, *but*, taking Rilke's advice made an immediate difference.

At all costs, I have found it important to keep my energy positive. Otherwise I will *repel the positive things that are on their way to me.* I have far too much past experience of succumbing to negativity, anger, worry, self-hatred, or discontent and *repelling all that is strong, striving, and bright.* (And it never did me any good at all.)

January 9

What Are You Leaving Behind?

As I was driving behind an overloaded trash truck on a cold and rainy day, discarded items kept blowing out and landing on my car. Before I was able to get into another lane, a full, dirty diaper hit my windshield, blocking my view and spreading its wealth. My wipers only made things worse. Besides the *ick* factor, it was dangerously distracting.

But the experience was a graphic illustration of what I have unwittingly done to the people *behind me* in my everyday life. Anger, gossip, negativity, discontent, and fear basically have the same effect as the dirty diaper on the windshield.

Starting today, I will be careful how I talk about life, politics, the world, our future, and my challenges.

I've learned that people will forget what you said, people will forget what you did, but people will never forget how you made them feel.

—*Maya Angelou*

January 10

What Is Your *Real* Work?

This morning, I hurried through my meditation, stressed about getting to my projects. Then, it struck me how funny this was. *To see more clearly, connect more fully to the pure and complete energy source is the real project.*

How silly humans can be! We stress over the *very* few things that we know about, while God is moving over all with complete awareness and perfect intent. My *only task* today is to connect to that knowledge and awareness. My life will then be guided and drawn to the *real* work. The simplicity of this single responsibility brings me joy and stops my stress, guilt, frustration, and worry.

And this is the coolest part: *joy moves me to success faster than any other emotion.*

January 11

Need a Partner?

If you could partner with the creator of snowflakes, would you?

If you could partner with the most insightful person in the universe, would you?

If you could partner with the most experienced person in the universe, would you?

If you could partner with the creator of love, would you?

And if you did, would you be able to relax more about your life and your future?

Would you be able to enjoy the sunlight, the acorns, and the breeze more?

Just asking because 1.11 is a perfect day to start.

"My yoke is easy and my burden is light."

—Matthew 11:30

January 12

The World Needs Me

May is a physically challenged, middle-aged grocery store cashier with a severely deformed hand, and she brought me—and probably many other people—*total* joy yesterday.

All May had to do was bring her *entire self* to work—and she did. She *really saw* the people around her and *really talked* to them. She *engaged* people around her and made them laugh. May was entirely delightful—just the way she was.

From the looks of her limp, May probably didn't feel great. From the look of her two-fingered hand, May's job probably was not the easiest job for her. But you would never know it!

More than anything, the world needs people like May—just the way they are.

Seriously? Lighten Up!

I am *light* today without the burden of regret for yesterday. I am *light* with forgiveness and joy. I am *light* without self-doubt about things I might have changed. I am thankful for all.

Not so long ago—just last year—I would have been dragging around my imperfections, heavy as a ball and chain. But today I realize that *I am transient* and *all things are transient*. I take myself less seriously and my calling more seriously. I will be *light*. And I will achieve all that I have been given the hope and talent to achieve. All.

Oh, you who change earth into gold…change my mistakes and forgetfulness into knowledge.

—*Rumi*

January 14

Expensive Mistakes

Yesterday, I made two expensive mistakes. I am a frugal person, and I hate inefficiencies. But *no mistake is as expensive as deciding not to be completely present in this moment.*

My family tried to teach me this lesson for years, reminding me that efficiency was not as important as *they* were. I was a slow learner. They paid the price many times, when I made them miserable for *my* oversights, wrong decisions, and accidents.

Today, I decide to concentrate on the good I can do right now—not the good I should have done before. If I don't forgive myself for my own mistakes, I will not be able to forgive others for theirs.

Face everything with love, as your mind dissolves in God.

- Lalla, fourteenth century North Indian Mystic
(Braybrooke 2001)

Stop Conflict and Pain

In a hotel concierge lounge, I greeted the frowning attendant kindly with, "Looks like you're having a hard day," which promptly backfired.

In response, he yelled, "How could you know that? You haven't been in here for five minutes. You don't know anything."

The entire room of people grew quiet, and even though I was tempted to feel embarrassed, instead, I responded, "I'm so sorry. My intention was to show interest and cheer you up."

He then said, "I'm doing just fine without your help."

In the past, I would have fretted about what I had done wrong or what he had done wrong. Now, I'm okay just remembering Marianne Williamson's advice in *Return to Love:*

"All that is not love is a call to love."

January 16

Stiff Neck for Nothing

This morning, I woke up with a stiff neck and shoulder because *yesterday* I allowed myself to stress about a forty-minute line at the post office. (I had told my husband, Bernie, that I would meet him during his run and finish the distance with him. I had no way to contact him and thought my delay was going to cause an inconvenience.)

But my timing worked out perfectly. The stress, neck and shoulder pain, *and the indigestion* were all unnecessary.

Same song, different verse: *there is never a good reason to be in a place that is not peace.*

At times, the stakes are, and will be, *much higher.* Learning to be peaceful today in *all* of our circumstances will yield big dividends, including better health tomorrow.

January 17

Alive!

I am alive. I breathe with refreshing pleasure. I move to the rhythm of my heart, which beats without pain or resistance. My eyes move and collect beauty without effort. I am aware of the light, air, and fragrance around me, encasing me as if in a womb of nourishment and protection. I sit erect, supported with the joy of purpose. I look at the future with resolve and courage. I smile with awareness of the grace available for each day.

I drink pure water, I read, I work on a laptop, I communicate with friends around the world, and I rejoice in all these luxuries. And I ask, *how can I use my gifts for others who do not know these luxuries?*

January 18

No Permission Needed

I love this Howard Thurman quote: "Don't ask what the world needs. Ask what makes you come alive, and go do it. Because what the world needs are people who have come alive."

I can always make excuses about how "someone else is already doing" what I think it is I want to do. I say to myself, "It's no use, my contribution won't be noticed" or "There's already a book about that." *But* this Howard Thurman quote completely changes my focus to *what makes me feel alive.*

(Thirty years ago, I said to myself, "I wish I could make a living writing, speaking, and sharing my opinion." If I had only known that that was all the permission I needed.)

January 19

I Am Good Fortune!

I ask not good fortune, I myself am good fortune. Henceforth I whimper no more, postpone no more, need nothing … strong and content I travel the open road.

-*Walt Whitman* (Whitman 1992)

Walt Whitman had it right! And what a breakthrough it was for me to realize that I *already* had everything I needed, as well. What a feeling of power. No more whimpering. No more complaining. Strong and content, I now travel the open road.

Let go of the anxiety about what you *don't* have. Latch on to joy. Everything you need will find you. No matter what your circumstances, *this feeling of completeness* has to come first, *before anything else* you think you might need.

Optimism is moral courage. You cannot thrive without it!

January 20

Relaxed State of Expectancy

Florence Scovel Shinn used the term "relaxed state of expectancy" in her (1940!) book, *The Secret Door to Success*. Like so many other modern *and* ancient sages, she has shown me how my past prayers were more begging than receiving, more trying to generate faith rather than relaxing in the joyful awareness of God's care for me—and how, as a result, I had unknowingly built a wall between myself and the help I requested.

Today, I take her advice. I am in a relaxed state of expectancy. I acknowledge my divine right to the support of the *entire universe*. I do not fear, fret, doubt, or bemoan my circumstances. My *joy* is a positive magnet, attracting *all* that I desire.

January 21

Your Word Is Your Wand

Hudson Taylor lost his wife and newborn in childbirth, and at the same time, an older child died of malaria. His missionary work in China was failing, and he was all alone in a strange country. If that wasn't enough, he also became deathly ill with malaria.

His journal said that he felt completely forsaken—until he started to repeat the Bible verse, John 6:35, over and over again: "He who comes to Me will *never hunger,* and he who believes in Me will *never thirst.*" After a few minutes with this simple exercise, Hudson Taylor said that he felt *happier than he had ever felt in his entire life!*

Florence Scovel Shinn wrote a book in 1929 entitled *Your Word is Your Wand.* I think that this story validates the concept.

January 22

Conquering Hell

My fifty-year-old neighbor, Mabry, was accidentally shot by his cousin, causing him to become a quadriplegic, when he was fifteen years old. His cousin never apologized. I asked him why he had such a good attitude about life in spite of his tragic situation, and he said, "One day, I realized I was going to be paralyzed whether I was happy or sad about it. It was a lot easier to be paralyzed when I was happy, so I quit being angry and have had a remarkable life since."

Life will throw us into hell at times. We have power to conquer even there.

Mabry inspired me to use that power.

A Suicide Every Six Minutes

I've contemplated it, too. Some of you never have, and I'm glad of that. My friend Ray Montgomery, who founded the Suicide Hotline in Dallas after his brother killed himself, always said, "Suicide is a permanent solution to a *temporary* problem."

A man who survived jumping off the Golden Gate Bridge said that his last thought before hitting the water was that *everything he was troubled about could be fixed*—except the fact that he had just jumped.

Our circumstances, though they often drive us to despair, contain a "Godly clarity" that we are not privy to. But if we hang around to see the rest of the story, we will be surprised, relieved, and impressed with how things work out—and how our lives serve a divinely unique purpose.

January 24

Healthy Detachment to the Rescue

Although I do not agree with all of Ayn Rand's philosophies, reading her books always reinforces my healthy detachment from the opinions of others, my confidence, *and* my contentment with *me*.

Researcher Brené Brown defined shame (in a TED.com speech) as *the fear of disconnect*. She identified three elements that work to remove *shame*:

1. accepting that that which makes us vulnerable makes us beautiful
2. having the courage to be imperfect
3. having the compassion to be kind to ourselves first

When we do all three of these, we can be *shameless:* completely free to love ourselves and others *without* the fear of rejection.

January 25

The Best Way to Deal with Random Unpleasantness

Since I cannot really *know* what is going on or the true significance of the seemingly random "stuff" that I sometimes have to wade through, I might as well be happy with all of it.

My friend Bill often quotes his grandmother's adage, "Nothing is ever as good as it looks or as bad as it seems."

He was right. I've been fooled many times before, so why not just let my worry go, relax about what *is,* and be surprised with the outcome?

Everything can change! Let dark Fate rule as it pleases. Be courageous! On the steepest track, trust in God! Ascend, despite crashing waves and weathers. Brave, like Caesar in his ship.

—*Fredrich von Mattisson* (Braybrooke 2001)

Yea!

Dishonesty Hurts More than Honesty

Prefer the truth and right by which you seem *to lose, to the falsehood and wrong by which you* seem *to gain.* —Maimonides

If you have to be dishonest in order to save your life, the price may be too high; *whatever* you may lose by choosing integrity is *better lost.*

As I type this, I vividly remember an incident that occurred when I was seven. While visiting a schoolmate's home, her mother called from the kitchen, asking if I was in her daughter's room. She meant *her room at school.* I answered, "Yes," thinking she was inquiring about her bedroom. I was too ashamed to admit I had misunderstood, so I made up a big, elaborate lie.

After that, lying to avoid owning mistakes became my *modus operandi.*

And, this method of dealing with the fear of being mocked or shamed was to cost me my integrity for many years to come.

January 27

Lost in the Universe?

My friend Maryanne told me that, when she was seven years old, she got separated from her family at Six Flags Over Texas. The experience was still a vivid, painful memory. She had despaired, thinking that her parents had so many children that they would not miss her. We laughed about it and then talked about *the reality of feeling invisible and insignificant.*

Many of us, at a very deep level, have felt similarly lost in the universe.

Today, I know that no life is ever forgotten or discounted. I now recognize my Creator's passionate desire and ability to keep track of *all* the children. Not one is insignificant—not even me.

You and I have unique and irreplaceable value—even more than Maryanne had to her parents.

January 28

We Are a Composite of Gifts

Several years ago, my friend Brent, who happens to be a personal trainer, helped me work on my posture. Now, every day when I pull in my abdominal muscles and throw my shoulders back, Brent deserves the credit.

(And what a helpful gift this has turned out to be. I didn't even know my posture was poor!)

When I see, wear, touch, or think of a gift or encouraging word I have been given, I also think of the giver and pray for that person—wherever he or she is.

(By the way, this is how I pray without ceasing.)

We are all a composite of *so many* gifts. Don't forget to be grateful. *What a gift it is to the giver!*

January 29

A Posture of Triumph!

Speaking of *posture*—

When my friend Jan and I attended a Tony Robbins seminar several years ago, Tony spent hours using Neuro Linguistic Programming (NLP) techniques to help us take on a *posture of triumph*. Before we walked on hot coals, we trained our minds and bodies to feel and act successful. It worked.

And it still works when I feel discouraged or depressed. I sit or stand as erect as I possibly can. I think of my most proud moment. I move my body as if I am there: joyful, victorious, elated, and bursting with confidence! I laugh at my challenges. I say out loud how happy and successful I am. It may feel and look funny at first—but not for long, because my body is able to *reprogram* my emotions!

January 30

The Terror of the Unknown

Cornelia "Corrie" ten Boom wrote about the courage she found during World War II, walking toward what she thought was to be her gas-chamber execution:

She remembered her first childhood trip to the crowded train station in Amsterdam. Corrie's father, understanding her terror of not knowing what to do or what was going to happen, had asked her not to worry about how to get the ticket, which train to board, or the confusion around them—but *to remember only one thing: to hold his hand.*

This image has given me courage and simple direction many times in my life. *I have only to concentrate on keeping my connection strong to my guide and keeper. Everything else takes care of itself.*

January 31

I Can Do That!

When I get bogged down in doubt, worry, or self-criticism, all comes back into proper perspective when I remember what my *real* responsibility is: *"—unless you become as a little child—"* (Matthew 18:3)

A child's responsibility is to play, trust, delight, love, grow, sing, and dance. Those things are easy to do! I was born doing these things.

It is never a child's responsibility to make things work out or to figure out how it is all going to work. A child just has to relax into the care of the caregiver. *When I do that first*, I open myself up to creativity, solutions, energy, and all the help the Universe has to give—and I become a joy to others, as well.

February

When Life Happens

No experience is a cause of success or failure. We do not suffer from the shock of our experiences, so-called trauma—but we make out of them just what suits our purposes.

—Alfred Adler

Prepared for Random Terror

The temporary nature of this life is frighteningly unpredictable. *Seemingly* random terror strikes. It will inevitably strike in your life as well, leaving loss as your companion. The only way to be prepared for this loss is to expect it, accept it, and live it *when it happens to someone else.*

To love your neighbor as yourself is to have *already* faced *the neighbor's* earthquake, flood, tornado, loss of a child, loss of parents, murder of a spouse, genocide, betrayal, bankruptcy, cancer, or hideous accident—to have grieved, in your being, with the sufferer—and then to have lived on with hope.

Ironically, this is *effective* fortification against terror.

And now, *strength and peace* are ready to replace that terror when it comes.

February 2

Suffering Repellant

The greatest cause of suffering is an utter lack of inner preparation.

—*Etty Hillesum, Holocaust victim*

From a Nazi death camp, Etty explained *inner preparation*: "When the sadness and fear overwhelm me, I fling myself down to my knees in the farthest corner of my inner life and stay there, kneeling, until the sky above looks sunny and clear again."

Many of us might "fling ourselves down" but that's all. We beg, plead, and worry and get up *in the same state.*

When we finally find that inner sanctuary and feel the immensity of our own value, there is a peace that no one can touch. Pain, death, betrayal, or loss will hurt but leave us intact.

Have you found that place?

February 3

Stopped Dead in Our Tracks

We are often stopped dead in our tracks by *stuff:* weather, failed technology, traffic, intestinal pains, or lost keys, for example. When *stuff* happens, there is nothing to do but trust that the timing is somehow perfect. The Buddhists say, "God is trying to keep us out of the-way so that something beautiful may be born."

Following a late-night flight home, I found myself at the airport without my car keys. At that point, I had a choice to make. I could fret about the cab expense and the complicated inconvenience of getting a new key and leaving my car there, *or,* I could enjoy the ride home, happy that my seventy-dollar fare was the taxi driver's profit for a very long, cold evening of work.

Giving thanks for the moment is the only way to glimpse eternity.

February 4

Am I Valuable?

Recently I witnessed a screaming mother *devastate* her five-year-old daughter. It reminded me of the rejection and insecurity I, too, felt growing up with an overwrought, angry mother.

It also reminded me of a haunting incident I had seen on a train in Melbourne, Australia. A distracted mother was yelling at, jerking, and belittling her small boys. I tried to show them kindness, and one boy looked at me with hatred in his eyes. The other buried his head with shame, desperately grasping his brother for comfort.

Their destinies could almost be predicted—*unless someone comes into their lives and shows them their irreplaceable value.*

I am thankful for those who have done that for me.

February 5

Just Show Up—Without the Agenda

I told my nephew about my lost car-key incident, hoping that it would inspire him not to worry about small stuff, as he often does. I set the stage: in the deserted airport after midnight, icy roads, too late to call anyone for help, knowing a taxi would cost too much, realizing my key was lost and could only be replaced by a dealer for three hundred dollars, the dealer who wouldn't be open until seven the next morning. I then asked what he would have done. He responded, "Me or Jesus?"

As I sat there, speechless, I realized that sometimes our lessons are *just* for ourselves and that's okay.

He then quoted a scene from the movie *Dumb and Dumber* to me.

February 6

Tell Yourself How It's Going to Be!

Tomorrow is a new day. You shall begin it serenely and with too high a spirit to be encumbered by your old nonsense.

—*Ralph Waldo Emerson*

I'm glad Emerson understood the concept of *our old nonsense* and the need of a high spirit to combat it.

He just told himself how it was gonna be.

It may have taken me years to figure this out, but I now know I *can* tell myself how it's going to be. I decide. Not my circumstances. Not my friends, not my family, nor strangers. Not the past, not the future. I decide right now what I want and live it—with power and confidence.

We were born to use our amazing power.

Try it and see what happens.

February 7

Forgive the Flaws

My nephew called me recently and commented, with uplifting assurance, "Pam, after spending the snow days with my grandparents, I realize that *who I am is not all my fault.*"

After a good laugh, his revelation reminded me of the talk I had had with our son in the aftermath of divorce. I said to him, "Hudson, I apologize for the ways we have screwed up your life."

Hudson responded with his particular brand of insight, "Oh, Mom, it's okay. We all screw each other up."

And, isn't it true? All of us are doing the best we can with what we've got. And, sometimes, what we have is pretty limited. Once we accept this, it's easier to forgive ourselves *and* each other for the flaws.

February 8

I Am Not Powerless!

Frequently, when depression or frustration sets in, it's because something has made us feel powerless. I used to accept this message and moan about the plague of mediocrity and anonymity. I don't do that anymore.

Instead, I close my eyes and feel the power in my body, the current of life in my fingertips, the power of water in my veins. I listen to the power around me in the wind. I feel the power of the sun on my face. I see the power of life in the dormant trees and grass, in the clouds, and in the birds. And I remember that I inhabit this place of power for a purpose.

I have the power to make a difference today!

Let the challenge begin.

February 9

Rename Yourself

Rosamund Stone Zander, author and therapist, describes her practice as "giving people the tools to rename themselves and their circumstances."

Victor Frankl, in *Man's Search for Meaning*, attests that often, the difference between those who survived the concentration camps and those who didn't was the decision to see their suffering as purposeful for the future. They renamed their pain.

Many times, this is the most important step toward hope.

I was taught this approach during natural childbirth classes. Instead of calling the contractions *pain*, they were *a natural process helping me toward the birth*. Instead of resisting the contractions with fear, I could, as a result, welcome them and cooperate with them. What a difference it made.

Today I rename myself *Powerful*, and my circumstances, *Joy*.

February 10

More Options than *Either/Or*

Recently, I became upset because I didn't know how to handle a particular situation, and I ended up making a mess of a conversation. Afterward, I called myself a total screw-up. I went from feeling great to feeling worthless in nothing flat.

It seems that, when we evaluate conflict with our emotions, we often go from *A* to *C*, completely skipping *B* in the middle.

Either someone was:

A. caring, or

C. selfish

Overlooked Option B: struggling

Either I am:

A. nice, and I get walked-on, or

C. mean, and I make enemies

Overlooked Option B: setting boundaries and communicating honestly.

Either my life is:

A. cool, or

C. terrible

Overlooked Option B: an emerging miracle

Life is so much kinder if we *remember option B.*

Fighting or Resting?

Several years ago I had a business meeting with Jeanette George, the actress who played Corrie ten Boom in the movie, *The Hiding Place*. She related a prayer-meeting experience where, with desperation, she had said, "God, we are in so much trouble, I don't even know what to tell you to do."

After it came out of her mouth, she laughed heartily at the revelation in her words; *she had been playing God all along*. It was a turning point in her life when she finally got it; prayer isn't about instructing God, but rather *resting from doing things ourselves*.

What are your prayers like?

Come unto me you who are weary and heavy-laden ... —Jesus

Ache: The Temporary Resident

I wrote this personification of ache after a long stretch of sadness that gradually eased up and then was *just*—gone (without my immediate awareness). It's a reminder that *all* states are temporary.

Ache

He left sans announcement
I'm shocked to relay
That my breath came and went
Painlessly today
Without his consent
(And his shameful demand
That I pay him for it!)

I just checked the back room
And behind the door
But it's undeniably true
He isn't here anymore.
(Funny
That I didn't notice
His absence before.)

But, shhhh! Look, over there!
That new neighbor (so eerily familiar)
I can barely hear,
Talking about his cousin, Joy,
That I'll want to meet
What? She's in the neighborhood?
Just down the street?

Don't be the Victim of a Closed System

Every problem, every dilemma, every dead end we find ourselves facing in life only appears unsolvable inside a particular frame or point of view. Create another frame around the data, and problems vanish, while new opportunities appear.

—*Rosamund Stone Zander*

So much of the pain in my life (I can now see) was self-imposed. My construct for judging myself, others, what was bad, and what was good was *ridiculously* flawed.

What freedom there is in saying today, "I have never seen the entire picture before, and I probably don't see it now—and, I'm totally okay with that."

All will be good in the end.

February 14

Valentine from the Universe

I used to dislike Valentine's Day because it highlighted my feeling of being unloved or not connected with that "someone special." Even in those days, I wish I had been able to see the love messages all around me—such as the sight of a remarkable and vibrant red bird in the snow-covered, barren tree outside my back door on Valentine's Day.

I pray you will see the hope and Valentine's Day messages surrounding you today.

We waste time looking for the perfect lover instead of creating the perfect love.

—*Tom Robbins*

Who Knows the Impact of One Life?

While in Little Rock, I was overwhelmed with a sense of my mother's presence. It was here that she was married the first time at the age of thirteen, and the fifth time at the age of twenty-six. It was here that she brought us to live with her parents, after divorcing her sixth husband. It was here that she was born. And, it was here, last year, where a woman in my audience said she had read my mother's obituary and it had made a difference in her life.

My mother came out of poverty and raised five children, retaining her tenacious sense of humor. She was spunky, often cantankerous, *and an unforgettable woman.*

As Charles Dickens commented about the obscure cleaning woman who had adopted an orphan in *Our Mutual Friend*: "No life is wasted that has lightened the load of another."

February 16

Change Your Life

For many years, I felt completely hopeless. A friend of mine said, "Change your life."

I said, "Yeah, right. That's easy for you to say. You are a retired pilot; you have lots of residual income, a wealthy wife, and no kids. I work sixty hours a week and have no savings and no college degree. I have a sick husband, three kids, a dependent mother with Alzheimer's, and a sister dying of cancer."

He said, "Change your life."

I hated to admit it, but he was right.

I went back to school, finished a degree, quit my job, and started my own business. I promptly went into deep debt (which is now completely paid off) and, today, am in love with my life.

There is *always* hope.

February 17

Thoreau Said It ...

I learned this, at least, by my experiment; that if one advances confidently in the direction of his dreams, and endeavors to live the life which he has imagined, he will meet with a success unexpected in common hours.

—*Henry David Thoreau*

The comments I received after I posted *Change Your Life* had to do with time.

- "Change takes a long time."
- "It doesn't happen overnight."
- "I tried."
- "Things didn't work out."

But if we are committed advancing in the direction of our dreams, hope *will* come and so will the help we need—when we *refuse to give up.*

And the feeling of success we have as we take steps, *even one baby step,* toward our dream is worth the risk.

(The angels will be applauding for you as ecstatic parents applaud the first steps of their children!)

February 18

A Hidden Door in *Every* Hell

There's a hidden door in every hell
That will not open
With banging, bashing, kicking, crying
Though everyone tries this first
We decide there is no door at all
Only seamless granite reinforced with steel
Until
In the gentle silence and surrender
The wall becomes soft to the touch
And yields the door

An old Chinese proverb says, *a man without a smiling face must not open a shop.*

This is true with our daily lives as well. Until we are in that place of joy, contentment, and faith, we are not presentable.

But it is equally true that without joy, contentment, and faith, we really *cannot* open the "shop" of our life. The door will be closed to us.

February 19

Someone Needs You to Endure

Earnest Shackleton scaled an icy mountain without proper gear, climbing for thirty-six hours without adequate food and water—after seventeen months of battling treacherous conditions in the Antarctic.

He kept going because he knew that if he gave up, his twenty-eight men would perish without hope.

Fortunately, he did not give up and the universe met his spirit of determination with the energy he needed to survive—and ultimately rescue his men.

I was thinking about this while trying to endure the final hills of a five-kilometer run on Saturday. Okay, I know that it is almost sacrilegious to compare the two scenarios, but my real epiphany concerned how I was giving up on a project that could potentially be a lifeline for many people. I went home after the race with new incentive and renewed energy to work for the sake of those who would not get the benefit of my gift if I continued to take the easy way out.

February 20

Tenaciously Me

There is vitality, a life force, an energy ... and if you block it, it will never exist through any other medium and it will be lost. The world will not have it. It is not your business to determine how good it is nor how valuable nor how it compares with other expressions. It is your business to keep it yours clearly and directly, to keep the channel open.

—*Martha Graham*

Knowing this not only helps me to appreciate and respect myself, it also gives me a sense of urgency to allow nothing to stop me. There are people who need *my* voice and who will hear their message from only my voice—*no matter what I think of my voice.*

I simply need to be myself *with tenacity.*

February 21

Wake Up—And Say Yes!

An urging, a voice inside, a recurring memory or dream—all are trying to wake us up to something.

We have ignored the messages before and regretted it.

We have discounted the medium or the messenger and said, "I know, but—," or, "I have no choice," or "What if things go wrong?"

We have tried to understand our future in the construct of our past.

Our future is not asking for our excuses. Excuses do not work in the construct of possibility that has been waiting a long time for us.

My life finally changed when I asked, "What's the worst that can happen if I take the risk?" *Not one* of the outcomes was worse than my current situation.

Today, I promise to listen.

February 22

Help from Heroes

I wake up this morning *deliciously aware* that I am supported by those who have gone before me in faith: imperfect people *like me* who lived nobly in the face of doubt, suffering, and countless obstacles, determined to overcome.

This knowledge buoys me over the ambiguity of this world, with all its injustice and brutality, fortifying me when I am tempted to despair, complain, or give up.

I remember their triumph. I remember their accomplishments. I remember how their contributions changed the world and gave me hope.

Now, whatever my task, it won't be about *just making it through the day.* It will be about much more.

Thank you, Lincoln, Shackleton, Mother Teresa, Corrie ten Boom, Joan of Arc and, of course, Dr. Seuss!

February 23

Moments of Painful Clarity

Sometimes, through the miracle of a dream or a random flash of vulnerability, I see myself through someone else's eyes. I can compare the revelation to the moment when I finally "see" myself in the mirror (instead of the image I want to see) and realize, *Gee, my clothes haven't shrunk, I really have gained weight.*

But, in that instant, something radical will happen to me. I will either writhe in self-hatred (covering my pain with all manner of creative camouflage) *or,* I will change my habits.

As painful as it is, these are magic moments in my life; moments when I grow up, when I become kinder and better, and when I become the person *I thought I already was.*

February 24

More Moments of Painful Clarity

I will not writhe in self-hatred after a moment of painful clarity if I realize that my *"new"* revelation is not new to anyone else!

People in my life have already seen my flaws. Maybe they were hoping that someday I would notice them, so that they would not have to hurt my feelings by bringing them up. Or maybe they had already tried to point them out, but I wasn't listening. Or maybe, they had already accepted me in spite of these flaws.

I was likely the last one to notice the flaws, so I don't have to fret about it. I merely have to accept myself *just as I am.*

February 25

Gratitude Magic Act

Sometimes, I can't find a thankful thought anywhere. The world seems too troubled, my life seems too complicated, and (seemingly) stupid stuff just keeps happening.

It's in those times that I have to "work" gratitude until it becomes real. I have to *notice* the Internet (what a convenience), and *my teeth* (a friend just paid for *bovine* implants), and *my eyes* (I was blind at one time, after an accident), and *my hair* (my friend, Carolyn, was *scalped* in a tornado and spent years in hospitals to get hair again). Then, *Voila! Gratitude appears.*

When you force gratitude
it is a wall
but, maybe it is a seed
sprouting beside the wall
maybe it yields a vine
that climbs
until it reaches the other side:
the open sky
the healing breeze
the living spring
the spirit call

February 26

Every Atom of Hatred

Every atom of hatred we add to this world makes the world more inhospitable.

—*Etty Hillesum*

Etty Hillesum died in a concentration camp at the age of twenty-nine. Her entire brilliant family was killed as well. But Etty was determined not to hate the Germans *because of the belief reflected in this quote.* As a result she became "the thinking and healing heart" in the barracks and is now well known as one of the most influential women of all time. At the end of her short life she said, "In spite of everything, life is beautiful."

We all have temptations to hate, resent, or hold grudges. If we give in, we punish ourselves *and* the rest of the world.

Today, let's choose to make this world more hospitable.

February 27

Just As *She Was*

My mother was married at least nine times and never really learned patience. At the end of her life, along with the challenge of dementia, she was mostly cantankerous and discontent. Being her primary caregiver was a life-consuming challenge—until I found her journal. In it I found this entry:

"I just want someone to understand me, love me, and accept me for who I am ..."

It could have been my journal. I had never before seen *my mother* in this context. Afterward, I made it my goal to listen, love, and delight in her. I began to accept her *just as she was.* I quit judging her and correcting her.

The improvement in our relationship was immediate—*and dramatic.*

Simple formula. Universal application.

February 28

Vocabulary Deletion

"I don't need this right now" used to be my response when seemingly random unpleasantness happened to me.

But no longer.

In natural childbirth classes many years ago, I learned this technique: *instead of resisting the painful contractions, tensing with fear, or concentrating on the pain, the contractions were to be accepted as a natural part of the process. Cooperating with the pain caused the birth to come faster and easier.*

When I apply this technique to life, I work with whatever happens, stay out of the PLOM (Poor Little Ole Me) Club, and give the situation my best with the confidence that all will work for good. As a result, not only do I enjoy my life more, *others enjoy my life more, too.*

March

Learning on the Job

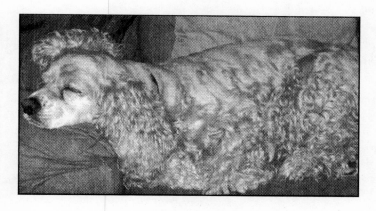

He who seeks rest finds boredom. He who seeks work finds rest.

—Dylan Thomas

This One Little Day

Those voices again.
Chattering about my demise
About my inability to take care of
This one little day
But I will rise with power
Above them all and say
This moment is mine
How dare you take it away?
Meet me at its end
I'll show you
What I've done
With this one little day

To my God a heart of flame, to my fellow-men a heart of love, to myself a heart of steel.

—St. Augustine

March 2

Tennis "Lessons"

Several years ago, Bill Belz, with much effort, taught me, *a total non-athlete*, to play tennis. Besides adding ten years to my life (probably), the game has taught me many life lessons.

- Don't think about who might be looking at you.
- Concentrate on loving the game.
- Keep your eye on the ball.
- Play one point at a time.
- Forget about the last point.
- Let go of the self-hatred for mistakes.
- Don't stress about winning; think only about being the best in this moment.

Until recently, I often sabotaged my game by feeling guilty about *playing* instead of helping someone, etc. Now, I know that this *play* has been and is a *very* important part of my life.

I hope you will *play* today—in whatever you do.

March 3

Getting out of a Narrow Place

Yesterday, in spite of my best intentions, I damaged a new client relationship. It was a breakdown in communication that I could have prevented by being a better *listener.*

My natural reaction to failures like this is to get defensive and justify myself, blaming the other party for misunderstanding me. If I do this, it puts me in a *restrictive and narrow* place, where I feel rejected, wronged, and demoralized.

So, yesterday, I went, instead, to the wide place of grace, where I was not misled by shame, where I could keep the experience in perspective, and chalk it up as a learning experience. And, wow, I could breathe again!

Life is so much easier when we don't take ourselves so seriously.

March 4

What Are You About?

A few years ago, I wrote a personal mission statement. It was a bit long and wordy, but it gave me the clarity I desperately needed.

Pam Boyd's mission is to use her creative, organizational, and motivational gifts to help connect people and make a positive difference in the world.

I recently shortened it to read *Give hope to the hopeless.*

Shortly afterward, in a leadership skills for women class, we spoke about the power of clarity in our lives. At the end, a manager for a hospice organization approached me with joy, "My mission statement is clear to me now. *Provide love for the unloved.*"

I had difficulty getting out of bed today—until I remembered her epiphany—and mine.

March 5

≥ (Greater Than or Equal To)

Before I hand over my day to unknown demands
That may ask more of me than I want to give
Before the centrifugal forces throw me hard
Against the outer wall of my existence
I come to you
Only you can help me see
That I am truly Greater than or Equal to
This day

Today is one of those days on which *everywhere* I look, I see work that has to be done, obstacles that have to be surmounted, problems that have to be solved. To avoid the usual spiral down into frustration and despair, I must take time to remember who I really am, the power I have been given, and the vision and promise of the future.

Now—*I'm ready.*

March 6

Escape!

It happens—those days that arrive drab, uninviting, and unpromising. Mostly they come because something unpleasant hovers on the horizon or because of some pain or some disappointment about myself or my circumstances.

That's when I have to borrow someone else's inspiration—just for a few minutes. Any visionary will do: a passionate musician, a motivational speaker, a preacher or mystic, a writer of fiction or non-fiction, an artist, friend, or poet. I grab onto their vision of hope, light, color, or strength and let it pull me out.

Lost in the space of hours and minutes of ache
Get out now before it's too late
Grab onto life
The whisper of dancing trees, playground noise, or ripening grapes
Just grab on now before it's too late

March 7

Completely Present

In this moment, I notice the feel of the computer keys on my fingertips.

In this moment, I notice that the computer corrects my errors automatically.

In this moment, I notice that I know how to read and write.

In this moment, I notice that I can quickly send a message across thousands of miles.

In this moment, I notice my eyes working.

In this moment, I notice that my breathing is happening automatically.

In this moment, I notice that my back doesn't hurt.

In this moment, I notice the way my clean clothes feel and smell.

In this moment, I remember the people who have helped me throughout my life.

In this moment—

March 8

Conduit of a Dream

A few days ago, stopped at a light, I looked up at the sky through my sunroof. There, as if in the middle of the clouds, was the cover of a book I had written. (The book was on the floor of my car and had reflected up into the sky!) It was a very odd sight that prompted me to remember the time when that book had been *just a dream.*

Thomas Edison always said that ideas came to him out of the sky. Einstein claims to have dreamed the theory of relativity. Picasso and Salvador Dali credit dreams for their masterpieces.

In dreams, we catch glimpses of a life larger than our own.

—Helen Keller

Today I want to be a conduit of my own *and* others' dreams.

March 9

No One Real Is Boring

I met a woman who told me she had shut down the intellectual part of herself in order to fit into her environment. She was stuck in a boring job, and her anxiety was glaringly obvious.

When we quit being *real,* our problems multiply. If we worry about being what we think we should be or become anxious about living up to someone else's expectations, we will *instantly* lose our personal power.

Tension is who you think you should be. Relaxation is who you are.

—*Chinese Proverb*

As American writer and thinker Gertrude Stein so eloquently said,

No one real is boring.

What a freeing thought this is. The world needs for you to be *you* today.

March 9

There's More than Meets Our Eye

I woke today from a disturbing and frightening dream: someone had made a wrong decision, costing the life of a member of my family.

Journalist Janine de Giovanni wrote *Madness Visible, A Memoir of War* about this nightmare for millions during the Balkan wars.

The Lovely Bones, by Alice Sebold, tells the painful story of a girl watching her murderer and her family from heaven, deciding between revenge or a broader view.

Life is often brutal and nonsensical. There will be times when each of us has to choose between bitterness or numbness and an acceptance that life is much more than meets our eye. Today, I want to be:

- aware of suffering
- active as a healer
- assured of a longer story that solves the puzzle

March 11

This, Too, Shall Pass

When I am weighed down by a pile-up of *yuck* (messages that are *not* uplifting), it helps me to remember that this state is only temporary. A good night's sleep or a change in focus will often move me away from that desert.

But if I fail to remember this and succumb to the mood of the moment, the state *will not be as temporary;* it will last much longer, and, inevitably, I will pull other people into the mood with me. Getting out will be a terrific struggle, and I will have wasted a lot of precious moments.

There is only one moment in time when it is essential to awaken. That moment is now.

—*Buddha*

March 12

Kneel and Kiss the Ground

The participant comments during a leadership workshop had turned into a gripe session until a woman in my class took the floor.

"I had a problem with negativity and discontentment at work until I lost my job. Having finally found another job, I now complete even the most menial task with joy and gratitude for the opportunity to work."

The mood of the group immediately changed.

All around us there are messages that *beg* us not to take *even the slightest thing* for granted. Listen to them.

There are hundreds of ways to kneel and kiss the ground.

—*Rumi*

Don't Play the Shame Game

I recently watched *Session 9*, a movie about the destructive power of shame. It is a very disturbing movie (not recommended unless you love psychological thrillers) but a powerful reminder to deal quickly with the pain of shame in our lives, before it spills out on someone else.

In my past, when I felt ashamed of something, I would launch a massive (mostly unconscious) cover-up that would drive me far away from authenticity, courage, and kindness. I became unkind because, unfortunately, when I was uncomfortable with myself, I balanced the scales by judging others.

But I am learning, instead, to recognize the symptoms of shame, laugh at my humanity, and *reject judgment of myself and others*.

What a difference it makes.

No one thrives with shame.

March 14

Go There Now!

*I saw Eternity the other night
Like a great Ring of pure endless light,
All calm, as it was bright ...*

—*Henry Vaughan*

When I dream of heaven, I wake up remembering *unearthly light* and a pervasive quiet peace. This poem captures the feeling and reminds me to go *right now* to that place of calm: to look out upon my troubles, my life and my future from the vantage point of eternity.

I had a similar feeling once after a dental procedure (ha-ha). But the very *temporal* nature of the medicated route is a problem.

The good news is that sages from all ages have told us that this experience of calm is available to any of us at any time in any place.

Go there now.

March 15

Shoulda, Coulda, Woulda

Yesterday was one of those days where I was continually prompted to think about what I *shoulda, coulda, and woulda* done differently, *if only—*

The effect on my psyche was subtle but deadly, draining off vital energy for creating, hoping, and working with joy.

This morning, I will look past the mistakes I made yesterday (and last week and last year) to the good I can do today.

Earth teach me regeneration
As the seed which rises in the spring.
Earth teach me to forget myself
As melted snow forgets its life.
Earth teach me to remember kindness (for others and myself)
As dry fields weep in the rain.

—Ute prayer

Miracle of Multiplication

The requirements of this day seem much larger than my abilities or resources. I can already feel the hot tension beginning in my right shoulder. To stay out of the cycle of hurry, worry, and inefficiency, I must stop my pinball movements from one thing to another and bring my resources, however small, as an offering.

All that I have is all that is required. I don't have to pretend to have more.

When my heart is at rest, the miracle of *multiplication* occurs.

Who trusts in God shall never be needy. God alone suffices.

—*St. Teresa of Avila*

March 17

Tree Messages—Against the Wind

My friend Barb, telling me about visiting the Biosphere in Arizona, explained that the trees there did not thrive. They had everything in the Biosphere *except wind*. Dealing with the wind, she expounded, stimulates and strengthens the growth of roots.

Later that day, another friend of mine, out of the blue, told me about the root systems of the amazing redwoods, explaining that their strength comes not only from the breadth of the root system but also by intertwining with the roots of other redwoods. *They hold on to each other's roots* against the wind.

This is about *the wind,* about latching onto the root systems of others who stand *against the wind,* and about *growing our own root systems* for others to latch onto.

Piece of Cake

Your ability to generate power is directly proportional to your ability to relax.

—David Allen (Getting Things Done)

One of the most important things I can do to *relax* is get to the place where I am *enough:* where I see that I am equal to my challenges, where I know I am who I am for a purpose, and where I am confident that I have access to all the resources I need. *Only then* can I relax.

What I say to myself will propel me to this place or *away* from it. I can say, "I'll never get all this done," or I can say, "Piece of cake!"

The choice I make will either shut my brain down or send it to work.

I choose cake!

March 19

Massive Ramifications

In the book *Return from Tomorrow* (George Richie's amazing after-death story), we meet a man who watched his wife and five children die at the hands of a firing squad.

The bereaved man said to George, "I had to decide whether to let myself hate the soldiers who had done this. As a lawyer, I had seen too often what hate could do to people's minds and bodies. Hate had just killed the six people who mattered most to me in the world. I decided then that I would spend the rest of my life loving every person I came in contact with."

The conversation confirmed George Richie's own supernatural experience, and consequently, how he would spend the rest of his life.

Profound conclusion. Massive ramifications.

March 20

Looking for the Longer Story

The tsunami in Japan, the war in Libya, bad things happening to good people, and unexpected health issues remind me that life is extremely transient and ever subject to change. I felt a little down about that until I took other factors into consideration.

- In *every* place of life there seems to be a special grace available for making it through.
- If we learn to care for others in their suffering as we care for ourselves, there is some redemption.
- There is a big picture and a longer story that I am not privy to.

Nathaniel Hawthorne had a wise saying about this last point:

"We sometimes congratulate ourselves at the moment of waking from a troubled dream; it may be so the moment after death."

March 21

Fish out of Water

CS Lewis, writing about humans being eternal creatures, made the point using fish:

"Fish, obviously, do not feel wet because water is their natural medium."

Lewis deducted from the observation that if time were *our* natural medium, we would not be oppressed by it, wake up thinking about it, or worry about it running out, as we so often do.

This information is important because it points to a longer story, a larger context, and a *much* bigger picture for our lives.

The temporal nature of our lives doesn't make sense because we are fish out of water. We have forgotten our *natural habitat* of eternity.

Today, I will remember to interpret the insanity in light of this information.

March 22

We Can Always Afford to Give

Today is another opportunity to give more than is expected, without fear of scarcity for myself.

I love the story about the widow whom Elisha asked for the last bit of food, intended as a final meal for her son. Instead of panicking, she prepared the meal for Elisha and, as a result, the food *never* ran out, and the relationship became an immense blessing for her family.

There is a temptation to protect our assets at all costs. But what do we gain if we protect our assets—and shrink our soul in the process?

Today, I will release whatever I am holding on to with confidence that all will come back to me when I need it.

March 23

People Are Not Props

As you walk in the world today, promise me; will you please promise me?

Will you promise to *see*?

Will you forget your agenda and promise to *see:*

- the people who cross your path?
- that not one is an accident?
- that not one is inconsequential?
- that not one is a prop on your stage?
- that *all* are *Me?*

Tread softly, for this is holy ground; it may be, could we look with seeing eyes, this spot we stand on is Paradise.

—*Christina Rossetti*

March 24

Let There Be Light

Although Andrew Carnegie's own education was not extraordinary, he believed (as Ben Franklin said) that *leaders are readers*. He built countless libraries, read voraciously, and sought out many, many mentors throughout his life. He was driven by a thirst for peace. He studied all religions and traveled extensively in an effort to *embrace and not judge* other cultures.

Today, *his spirit inspires me toward peace.* When I have a judgmental thought about people I do not know, I will seek out knowledge about those people. I will walk in their shoes, their homeland, and their challenges. I will *delight* and not judge. So that darkness will not be my guide, I will repeat the words written over the door of the Carnegie Library:

"Let there be light."

March 25

Fear of Disconnect

Author and researcher Brené Brown defined shame as *the fear of disconnect*. That makes sense to me because I spent much of my life *hiding*, lying, and pretending in an (often subconscious) effort to avoid the pain of disconnect.

Many years ago, an acquaintance told me that I seemed troubled. I denied it. I was bummed because I felt like a failure as a mother, but I didn't want her to know the details. She sensed something and told me that her son had recently been court-martialed in the army for dealing drugs.

What a difference her honesty made for me.

We are all connected.

But unless we are honest, present in the moment, and available to do so, *we won't know it.*

March 26

Traveler's Hope

Sometimes, when I am traveling on the other side of the world (or around the corner), I feel a sudden rise of anxiety about being utterly alone, totally anonymous, and completely unattached to familiar things. As I pray and look up at the moon, I remember that this is the moon of Joan of Arc, Abraham Lincoln, Victor Hugo, Pearl Buck, and Nelson Mandela.

I realize that this place has witnessed and supported the journeys of humans for centuries. I realize that there are mentors and angels for me and I have never been alone. I choose to accept their power and my mission.

As I travel through the night, protect me with a cloak of Heaven's shining might, moon's floating light, fire's passionate flare, wind's soaring wildness—

-A Portion of an Icelandic prayer (Braybrooke 2001)

March 27

Much is at Stake

Recently, a man in my management class told me his story:

When he was five, his father, while in a drunken bout of self-pity, shot himself. His mother, in despair, abandoned him and his two-year-old sister.

He then told me how a caring couple, intending to adopt a little girl, showed mercy and adopted them together. Their selfless choice totally changed his life. He has gone on to be a blessing to many others as a result.

The choices I make are also choices for people in my path. Many of them I don't even know, *but they will live with my choices.*

I must live each day as if much is at stake—because *it is.*

March 28

The X-Factor

I'm not talking about the TV show. I'm talking about you and me living the life we were created to live: a life of *Xtraodinary* power and presence!

The X-Factor in life is the same as the X-Factor in performing: that thing that sets us apart from everyone else. It is our gift, our unique voice, wildly used with Xtraordinary confidence and presence in this world.

We've got it. We may have to unbury it, dust it off, reclaim it, and disengage it from the tentacles of fear, disappointment, and disillusionment that have concealed it from the world, but it is there.

And the world needs our X-Factor today.

After all, according to Robert Louis Stevenson, life is *"a thing to be dashingly used and cheerfully hazarded ..."* (Stevenson 2011)

March 29

From the Biggest Chicken Ever

The fear of death follows from the fear of life. A person who lives fully is prepared to die at any time.

—*Mark Twain*

What freedom this quote contains! A person who *lives fully* is not afraid of death—*or of life*. Bring it on! Have confidence in the strength God has given. Have confidence that all happens for a reason. Have confidence that *you are enough*.

When we hear ourselves say, "I'm afraid that_____," whatever comes after this phrase doesn't matter. Own it for what it is—*a life thief.*

Face the fear. Give up preconceived notions about what must be (with our circumstances, children, economy, health, etc.). Start creating strength, alternatives, and joy, versus a construct of anxiety.

Courageously,

Pam Boyd, *Reformed* Biggest Chicken Ever

March 30

"Strange Things are Happenin' to Me"

A few years ago, I thought my life was over. Nothing had turned out as I had envisioned. I felt as if I were on a precipice overlooking a hopeless descent.

Today I hear the message of spring:

It may look dead, desolate, gone, sad, and defeated but appearances are deceiving. Just wait until I show you the magic of transformation. Just wait until I reveal the hidden life, the hidden hope, the hidden color, and the hidden blossom that lives in the dark of death.

Strange. That message has been repeated to me, in loud symphonic stereo every year of my entire life—and I am just now hearing it.

March 31

The Power of Delight at Work

Any relationship can be altered or even revived if judgment is replaced with delight. I don't know about you, but I don't like being around someone who judges me. I can feel the space closing in around me, and I want to get out and breathe.

Sometimes, in the business world, we blame our lack of clout, relationship, or ability to advance on office politics or some other arbitrary condition, when it is merely that our bosses sense our judgment (criticism, cynicism, or insincerity) and not our delight.

In most cases, when we bring our authentic selves to work with a sincere gratitude for our jobs and for our coworkers (exchanging judgment for delight), improved relationships and work conditions follow.

April

Your Impact

You can have an impact anywhere you are.

—*Tony Dungy*

April 1

It's a Great Day; Change Someone's Energy!

Here are the rules.

1. Make someone laugh today.
2. Don't take yourself so seriously.
3. Admit that being a "fool" is part of life.
4. Own the foolish things you've done.
5. Don't be fooled twice.
6. Have fun.

Not a bad list for *every day*. Change someone's energy today!

Happy April Fools' Day!

April 2

Chin-Ning Chu

In her book, *Thick Face, Black Heart,* Asian-American best-selling author Chin-Ning Chu is painfully honest about her life:

"One morning, years ago, I woke up with an overwhelming feeling of aloneness overtaking my soul. I felt as if my spirit were covered by layers of dark clouds. I lived but made no difference to the world—I stood alone in the pit of my soul. I felt the world could do very well without me. I didn't see any hope, only despair. Then I picked up a book entitled *Soaring—*"

In that book, Chu heard the message that if one is destined for great accomplishments, the preparation for the journey will be extensive. She embraced the message and went on to make a difference.

Today, her endurance encourages *me.*

April 3

Prepare for Departure

Twenty minutes into an already delayed flight, the turbulence was so bad that the plane experienced radical altitude changes. The flight attendants were thrown down in the aisle and forced to crawl to reach the back of the plane. Then, the young pilot came on the intercom:

"Flight attendants, prepare for *departure*."

There had already been screams, now there was palpable silence. *Prepare for departure?* Was it a Freudian slip? Did he know something we only suspected?

Well, I prepared for departure: I prayed for my family, my uncompleted work, and someone to complete it.

Moments like these are good check-ups on our *peace level* and on what's *really* important.

After landing, no one complained about delayed luggage, I assure you.

April 4

When Did You Stop Seeing Me?

When did you stop seeing me?
Was it when life became more complicated
Than you planned?
Was it when you were disappointed?
Angry? Worried?
I just know it happened.
I didn't seem to be important to you anymore.
I went my way. You went yours.
Life became more about getting by
Than about joy.
I am the people in your life who need you
Your uniqueness, your laughter, your delight.
Please come back.
Promise to *see me*—and not the agenda.
I'll promise to *see you*.

It's easier to be God than to love God in others.

—*Dr. Henri Nouwen* (Nouwen 1979)

April 5

Your Work in the World

Last night, I kept dreaming of new ideas for bringing hope: dream after dream of making a difference in the world.

Sometimes I don't have *any* ideas. But when ideas do come, they come with a choice.

I can either feel overwhelmed, saying to myself, "You don't have time for any new ideas; you're not even doing well with the ideas you already have," or I can say, "Thank you, God, for new ideas. I don't know how to use these ideas and make them a reality, but I'm willing to be a conduit of hope. Give me a way to utilize them."

Your work is to discover your work and then with all your heart give yourself to it.

—*Buddha*

April 6

Staying Out of the Drama Trap

It has taken me decades to learn how to treat good news and bad news the same.

In the past, when I received accolades and everything seemed wonderful I would soar. Then, the next day, when things didn't go so well, I'd crash and splatter. Now, I know, whether the news is good or bad, it is always an incomplete picture and a *temporary* state.

There is so much more going on than our limited vision could ever reveal to us. So we can save our energy and trust that all will work out in the end.

When we practice this type of healthy detachment from outward circumstances, we are saved from the dreaded drama trap.

April 7

Tear-Down Stage

To update our house, we have to tear it apart. We know this has to happen. We endure the brutal ripping out, pulling up, and knocking down because we understand the destruction will soon be replaced with much more beautiful surroundings. We accept the process.

So, why can't I remember this when my *life* is being torn down? Instead, I whine, whimper, curse, despair, and fret. I lose all perspective and start believing that this tear-down stage is my permanent state. I forget that something wonderful is coming afterward.

"Wow, you seem different!"

"Yes, I've been remodeled."

Unless a grain of wheat falls into the earth and dies, it remains alone. But if it dies, it bears much fruit.

—*Jesus*

April 8

Messy Lives

If the life of someone you love looks like a mess right now, it might be because they are in the tear-down stage of remodeling.

If I judge the value of a house by how it looks during this stage of the remodel process, I will be extremely discouraged. Instead, I will wait patiently, with anticipation, until it is complete before I judge its worth.

Some of you probably remember the PBPGINFWMY (Please-be-patient-God-is-not-finished-with-me-yet) buttons from the Jesus Movement. I wore one proudly and thought the message was very cool, but I had no idea what the button really meant and what I was in for!

Construction and *reconstruction* are messy stuff.

April 9

Useful Memories of Local "Flavor"

I have met too many wonderfully unique and delightful people (many of them living in obscure places, doing obscure and seemingly unimportant jobs) to ever think that life is meaningless. I'm talking about people like Jimmy Don from Smackover, Arkansas; Ed from Mexia, Texas; and Anne from Bangor, Maine, who totally brightened my day by simply being themselves.

When the chaos and random insanity of this life shatters my faith, I find refreshment in the memory of these encounters, as I do in the stored sensations of misty mornings, majestic mountains, and vast oceans. I now *understand* the expression, salt-of-the-earth, because these people have completely changed the flavor of an ordinary day and my earthly experience.

Such goodness, evil can *never* extinguish.

April 10

To be Present—Detach?

No matter where you are, make sure you are there.

—*Mahatma Gandhi*

Upon reading that quote, my first thought was, "Duh, not that profound." *But* practicing the quote is quite another story.

My friend Lesley said she was trying not to lose the joy of today for fear of tomorrow—and all the expected layoffs. I know! It's hard to be peaceful and present when you feel a threat of losing something very important to you.

That's why *the art of detachment,* ironically, is essential to being complete present. Chin-Ning Chu, in *Thick Face, Black Heart,* teaches detachment from our little ego and attachment to the gigantic divine ego—essentially, letting go of our own picture of how things need to be so we will relax into the bigger picture.

Only then can we *really* be there.

April 11

You Must be Present to Win

If I just make it through the day—so what?

So what if I did my little tasks and survived another day without a major crisis? Life has to be more than feeding and entertaining this body so that I can sleep and wake up to feed and entertain this body again.

When I live like this, racing through life to take care of my business, regardless of my accomplishments, I have missed the point. If I take the time to notice, the emptiness inside will become obvious to me.

But if I slow down to really *see* the people around me, to delight in their stories and their journeys, and to enter their world and honor their existence, life becomes *so much more.*

April 12

See the Story; Make the Movie

While in a crowd of people, I make a point to see each face and imagine the potential movie of each person's life. That keeps me from thinking of them as simply obstacles in my way.

When we watch a movie, we purposely focus outside ourselves and on someone else's story for a couple of hours, totally losing ourselves in the struggles, emotions, and personal development of these strangers whom we just met on the screen! Characters in movies don't even have to be famous, amazing, or heroic—or even real!—for us to do this. We become completely enthralled in whatever is happening to them, regardless of how mundane. It's amazing.

So, maybe if we see *everyone* as an interesting story—as movie material—we will be more compassionate toward them.

April 13

Egoless People-Watching

Several years ago, I noticed that my people-watching was also *people-judging*. I was not only observing, I was sorting, comparing, and deciding—sometimes sentencing—but always with insufficient information.

I now realize that a sense of appreciation for the things I don't know about people puts people-watching on a totally different plane.

When I am generous with others, I am generous with myself. Generous people are refreshing to be around. Generosity starts with our thoughts.

Always give the benefit of a doubt to others. We never know the whole story.

April 14

It Doesn't Take Much

It doesn't take much for us to change someone else's energy *and* it doesn't take much for someone to change ours.

In Chicago, a woman in my seminar told me about waiting in a grocery store line behind an elderly woman. She said that the woman was complementing people, making eye contact with everyone, and finding out about them. The woman in my class said she was *amazed* at the difference this made and decided, "instead of thinking about my bills, my frustrations, how tired I am, or what's going to happen to me tomorrow, I'm going to focus on making lives around me just a little bit better."

When she came into my class, she did that for me.

April 15

What Is Associated with Your Name?

My friends Danny and Leslie Loftin recorded Danny's piano music for me. When I am out on the road, I play the CD while I am preparing to lead a seminar. The music takes me to a place of complete relaxation, appreciation, and peace. Now, I just have to see the CD with Danny's name on it, and the pleasant feelings begin.

This made me wonder what someone may feel when they see, hear, or think of my name. Do I bring music or noise? Am I associated with pain or with joy, with hope or with disappointment, with dread or anticipation?

I've got some work to do.

I love the name of honor, more than I fear death.

—*Julius Caesar*

April 16

Just what I Didn't Want to Hear ...

A man sat down beside me on an airplane and said, "I've had a day from hell, and I will tell you all about it as soon as I get settled."

Great.

He proceeded to monologue for the balance of the trip. Although it was almost midnight and my day had been challenging as well, I reverenced his journey by giving my attention. But when I showed interest by asking a clarifying question, he jumped onto another tangent and *rode it all the way home.*

It made me wonder about times I had done this to others.

Sometimes, we are so engrossed in our own stories, we fail to share the *airspace.* We may fail to ask ourselves, is something else on *their* mind right now?

April 17

Just Stop Running Around for a Minute—

I love it when my dog comes and sits quietly beside me while I work—and allows me to gently pet him, rather than running circles around me, trying to get me up to play or to get him something to eat.

Today, I decide to sit quietly beside my creator long enough to get the quiet attention, the gentle strokes, and the affirmation that I am loved, honored, and cared for. In this place, I am quietly aware of my beating heart that sustained me during the night, my incessant breath that nourishes me, and the inexplicable *life* that connects me to the giver of all life.

Like weary waves, thought follows upon thought, but the still depth beneath is all thine own.

—*George Macdonald*

April 18

The Right Face

When my son, Hudson, was five he said, "Mommy, that person has the right face."

I thought it was an odd thing to say, until I realized he wasn't talking about bone structure. He was talking about the smile.

A smile is a *welcome mat* for others.

If you don't smile, two out of three people, because of self-esteem issues, water-under-the-bridge issues, or their current challenges, are going to think you are angry, don't care, or don't like them.

If you don't think you have anything to smile about, take inventory.

A smile is a small thing to give. And, it's the beginning of a good day for you *and* for many people who are looking for *the right face.*

April 19

A Thousand Splendid Suns

A Thousand Splendid Suns, by Khaled Hosseini, is a novel about women in Afghanistan. It's one of those books that gets into your subconscious and affects the way you think about everything.

I put the book down, but I can't quit thinking about the awful things people bear and how critical it is for us (men and women) to passionately decide to love, forgive, and believe in ourselves and in our possibilities at all costs, regardless of our circumstances.

Choosing otherwise will pull us further down into a whirlpool of pain. We must choose to get out now—out of anything that is made of fear, resentment, hatred, negativity, or despair.

Our lives *and the lives of others* depend on it.

April 20

Self-Inflicted Penalties

Whenever I give in to fear or scarcity thinking *of any kind,* it brings a self-inflicted penalty with it. Usually, not only am I penalized, but people in my life are penalized as well.

It's funny how I completely "get this" when I read about other people doing it in a book, or see it happening in movies, or observe strangers, but I can't seem to see myself doing it.

But if I stand back as an observer of my own life, I might get a clearer picture of the tension and pain my own fear creates in the lives of others. When I release my fear and, instead, live in a place of abundance, what good it brings *to everyone!*

Oversight

I'm sorry I underrated your childhood chatter
And laughter
I'm sorry I didn't stop to hear it all
On my way to do whatever it was that I had to do
Now what was that?
What could have been as important as that childhood laugh?
Oh, yeah.
I was running to catch dinner
And myself
(Which I never caught until you were gone)
I'm sorry I didn't help you see how wonderful you already were
Because I didn't appreciate the wonder of me yet
And it's true
I couldn't do for you
What I hadn't yet done for me

April 22

The Day Done Right

I bring to You this day.
If I can't have it my way
Help me to see the day as it is meant to be
Never really owned or belonging to me.
The day I planned is merely an intern's version, a scribbled draft
Not hardly the reflection of Your time-perfected craft
Which ultimately unveils each day flawless and right,
Once I have surrendered my anxiety-ridden oversight.

April 23

As Sensitive as a Dog

I grew up knowing that dogs could smell fear. But animal behaviorists say that dogs can actually smell all emotions, not just fear. Recently, I've noticed when I am displaying affection, some other emotion, or any unusual behavior, my dog begins to sniff the air around me to determine what exactly is going on.

I've come to the conclusion that I could use this skill.

When I hurt someone's feelings, under-react, or over-react, it is frequently because I haven't *sniffed* out the situation enough and have missed what is really going on behind the words.

I will work today to be more *"scent*sitive," or at least, more sensitive. I owe this to the people in my life.

April 24

Little Minds Need Little Things to Occupy Them

When I was managing restaurants, I made a rule that gossip would no longer be tolerated. When I discussed the new rule with my assistant managers, Mike said, "Are you kidding me? Do you mean that we are not going to allow anyone to gossip, *even on their breaks?*"

When I answered yes, he responded, "So, what will they talk about?"

Our communication is often much more dysfunctional than we realize. But if we make a commitment not to say anything that we wouldn't want someone to overhear us say, what a difference it makes.

Always speak for intended as well as unintended audiences.

April 25

Stop "Fat People" Criticism

Almost daily, I hear "fat people" talked about, judged, condemned, and sentenced without a trial.

A friend of mine, who has struggled with weight gain all her life, says that overweight people experience more discrimination than any other group of people. I can believe it!

People who refuse to justify this type of criticism, do so because

- they may have had a weight problem before and know how challenging it is to overcome;
- they know, someday, they may also have a weight problem;
- they know that weight gain is often a side-effect of other medical problems;
- they understand the complex nature of addiction;
- they realize that, unlike other addictions, one can't just stop eating; or
- they are mature enough to know that we *all* have our *stuff*; some addictions are just easier to hide.

April 26

A Woman Who Had Loved and Had Been Loved Back

Khaled Hosseini, in *A Thousand Splendid Suns*, wrote this line for his main character as she headed toward execution. Her last peaceful thoughts were about her significance:

"She had loved and been loved back. Not so bad, she thought."

But this love had come at the very end of a painful life without love.

The message from the end of this book reminds me of *A Tale of Two Cities*, where Sydney Carton finds the ever-elusive love and redemption on his way to the guillotine. Many years ago, this scene made such an impact on me that I named my daughter, Sydney, after the Dickens character.

Love is worth living and dying for. Give it today *without any strings attached*.

Nothing is more important.

April 27

Trillions upon Trillions

My friend Mary called me a few days ago and told me to go outside and listen.

As I sat outside, I heard what she wanted me to hear: the celebration of birds and dancing leaves.

I also saw a million leaves representing trillions upon trillions of intricate life-giving systems. I started thinking about the cells' mitochondria and ribosomes and the veins that brought nutrients to the farthest cell in the farthest leaf. Then, I thought of my own body's micro universe of life.

Everywhere I turned, there were miracles: blades of grass, flowering plants, little insects, gentle breezes, a ball of light in the sky, billowing clouds, and my own senses to experience the miracles.

Sometimes this simple exercise of *paying attention* is the key to finding all that has been missing in our lives.

April 28

I May Be No Idol, but I Was Born to Belt It Out!

It could be the painkillers or it could be the soulful singing on American Idol, but right now, this moment, I am sure we all have a purpose!

American Idol judge, Babyface, commented that contestant James Durbin was born to sing Carole King's song—or maybe Carole King was born to write for James Durbin. The song said it all.

I may not be born to sing, but I was born to belt it out in some *other way*. I'm getting more sure about which way that is every day.

It strikes me, though, that if James Durbin worried about how weird his ears were and how he didn't look like anyone's idol, he may not have used his gift the way he did in the competition.

April 29

Miracle Cure

In his autobiography, publishing legend Edward Bok wrote about the untidy personal appearance of Robert Lewis Stevenson:

"Stevenson was an author whom it was better to read than to see. And yet his kindliness and gentleness more than offset the unattractiveness of his physical appearance."

Kindliness and gentleness are often a miracle cure for negative impressions.

If we have physical liabilities, first impressions have the power to kill our chances for work, relationships, etc., unless we bring the qualities of genuine kindliness and gentleness into play.

If I work at delighting in people around me, there is a guarantee: *my energy will attract delight to me,* regardless of my physical limitations.

April 30

I've Got the Power!

This morning, when I was trying to get out of bed with a back injury, I was braced for pain, subconsciously saying, "This is really gonna hurt."

When I caught myself, I changed my mantra to, "This is easy, I can do this," and Voila! My muscles relaxed, and I got out of bed with little pain.

This is only one small demonstration of the power of our words, and it reminded me of Zig Ziglar's motivational series, *Changing the Picture*. His simple recommendation was to look ourselves in the mirror *every day* and say things like, *I am fit, I am honorable, I am dependable, I am successful, etc.*

The simple concept of affirmations, taught by successful people all over the world, really works.

What are you saying to yourself today?

May
Sowing and Reaping

Results? Why, I have gotten a lot of results. I know several thousand things that don't work.

—*Thomas A. Edison*

May 1
Time for New Strategies

My friend Jan gave me Angeles Arrien's book, *The Second Half of Life*. Frankly, I was a little offended. (Gee, I'm not that old, am I?) But it really was a good book. Arrien made the point that when we age maturely, we will

- quit taking ourselves so seriously;
- take material things less seriously; and
- quit trying to change people.

We start recognizing the things that are *really* important, and we finally realize that we can't change anyone. We accept them as they are, delight in them just as they are, and quit trying to play God.

And when we quit trying to change people, ironically, *they often will want to change for us.* (This might be because we are not so annoying anymore).

May 2

Easier When You Smile?

After he ran the Oklahoma Memorial Half-Marathon in blustery rain and cold, Bernie told me he had an epiphany:

"Running is easier when you smile."

I think it is true. I just found out this week that moving around with a back injury is easier when you smile.

I know that going to work is easier when you smile.

Waking up in the morning is easier when you smile.

I can't think of anything that is not easier when you smile.

Try it. And let me know what you think.

I'm willing to be corrected.

I don't like being corrected, but, it's easier *when I smile.*

Embezzling Sanity and Abducting Peace

The documentary *Deep Water* chronicles Donald Crowhurst's 1968 attempt to sail solo around the world. The real story is about his breakdown of integrity, that was brought on by the fear of failure and defeat. He resorted to an elaborate cover-up that ultimately ended in complete and total devastation to himself and his family.

Horatio Alger defined integrity as a lack of lying, stealing, and cheating. Simple.

When we lie, steal, or cheat because we don't see any other way to save face or get what we think we so desperately need, the prize itself will steal what we really wanted: *happiness.*

Frantic grasping abducts peace, penalizes innocent parties, and, ultimately, takes our sanity.

To hold on to nothing is the root of happiness and peace.

—*Angeles Arrien*

May 4

Mending Relationships

We can change the dynamic of almost any relationship by setting our ego aside and asking the following three questions about the *other party*.

- *What do they want?* (Understand the very root of their pain.)
- *What do they do well?* (See them as valuable.)
- *What can I do to help them get what they want?* (No one will care about your agenda until they are sure that you care about theirs.)

Unfortunately, what most of us do is fixate on what *we* want, on what they should understand that *we* do well, and on what they should be doing to help *us* get what we want. But when both parties are stuck on their side of the story, nothing changes.

May 5

The Power of Self-Talk

When Dodie Osteen was told she had terminal liver cancer, she decided to live without cancer, whatever the cost. When the pain was unbearable, she visited others who were sick. She would not allow her family to help her with chores around the house. Sometimes in tears, she performed very difficult tasks, always saying to herself that she was healthy and was not dying of cancer.

A few months later, the tumors were gone.

Her approach was different from begging, pleading, crying to God about her cancer. She was *telling her body how it was going to be.* She took charge of her own energy, turning it into a healing machine.

Our thoughts create emotions. Our emotions create biological responses. The secret: *thoughts* become *things.*

May 6

Reluctant Positive-Thinking Convert

I used to resist all the power-of-positive-thinking hype.

Besides thinking it was a practice in self-delusion, I thought it distracted from faith in God. Now, I believe that our creator is begging us to use this creative power.

I often use a portion of the poem *Will* by American poet and author, Ella Wheeler Wilcox as a call to action:

There is no chance, no destiny, no fate,
Can circumvent or hinder or control
The firm resolve of a determined soul—

Why, even Death stands still,
And waits an hour sometimes for such a will.

                    -Ella Wheeler Wilcox (Wilcox 2007)

May 7

We Are Only as Sick as Our Secrets

If we want more pain, mental illness, and stress in life, we must

1. hide more stuff from people;
2. never tell the whole truth;
3. mask our weaknesses;
4. worry about what people would think of us *if they only knew*; and
5. pretend to be something we're not.

If we do these things long enough, we will

1. start to believe our own lies;
2. be confused about what truth really is;
3. never be completely free;
4. distrust and resent others; and
5. lose ourselves and, consequently, our unique gift to the world.

Life *turns on* when we decide to be authentic. And, ironically, all the things that we thought we would lose by doing so will, instead, come willingly to us.

May 8

Your Brain is Better than Google

—If you use it.

Many of us fret all day long about something and never get anywhere. We run circle after (unconscious, subconscious, and conscious) circle around it. We say things to ourselves like, "I don't know what to do," or "I can't believe this is happening to me," or "This is so bad," but we never really send our brain out to find the answer. (Even our prayers are riddled with repetitive despair.)

This behavior is like typing our problem on the Google search bar, over and over again, wording it in every way imaginable, but never hitting "enter" or "search."

Wired to solve problems for us, *our brain's "search" button is this: I know there is a solution. Help me find it.*

May 9

Oh Happy Day—with Secretariat

Oh Happy Day! I spent my Mother's Day over the Pacific Ocean, but had the *best* Mother's Day gift watching *Secretariat* on the plane. Some of it is so Hollywood, but the story is inspirational enough to cover for its weaknesses.

Here are the take-aways.

- Don't take no for an answer when you've got something good to offer. (I really needed this.)
- *Live* life!
- When you are born to run, you must run. Whatever you were born to do, you've gotta do it, whatever the cost. Go for broke—*even if your family thinks you are crazy.*

If you need a little inspiration today, *Secretariat* might *take you there!*

May 10

Andrew Carnegie's Simple Prescription

A sunny disposition is worth more than a fortune—the mind, like the body, can be moved from the shade into sunshine. Let us move it then!

—*Andrew Carnegie*

That's a big statement for Carnegie to make, since he understood the value of a fortune! But just in case you think he was too simplistic, he qualified his philosophy, "The only time one can't laugh trouble away is if it comes from one's own wrongdoing." Then, quoting Robert Burns: "Thine own reproach alone do fear."

In other words, whatever comes, it is imperative to

1. be true to your own conscience;
2. fix what you can fix;
3. stop worrying about anything else or anyone else's opinion; and
4. quickly move yourself into the sunshine.

Simple—but effective.

May 11

The Vise-Grip of the Dreaded Drama-Cycle

I watched Gwyneth Paltrow's convincing performance in the movie *Country Strong*, and came away with a strong admonition to resist being consumed alive by my own angst, guilt, regret, disappointment, or bitterness.

I don't want to sound overly simplistic, but I know I have the power to step out of the drama–cycle by rigorously moving my focus off myself and onto a *bigger picture*. Once I do that, people will respond differently to me, primarily because I am not consuming their lives with my stuff. And when people respond differently to me, I have less to be stressed about—and that shuts down the cycle.

I can either be in the *vise-grip of a vicious and relentless drama-cycle* or I can step into healing and hope.

I can choose.

May 12

A Still Place of Light

An excerpt of a prayer from Malling Abbey, Denmark:

Make me a still place of light
A still place of love
Your light radiating
Your love vibrating
Your touch and your healing
Far flung and near
To the myriads caught
In darkness, in sickness
In lostness, in fear—

What a hopeful depiction of what we can be to others. I like the image of this prayer. It reminds me that this is the destination.

My destination is not success. It is not a vacation. It is not health. It is not things. It is never places. My destination is a still place of light and love.

How simple life can be.

The Power of a Person Who Is a Still Place of Light and Love

Reading Andrew Carnegie's autobiography, I am impressed with the character, peace, love, joy, and hunger for life that his parents instilled in him as a child. Even when life was very cruel to the Carnegies, in their early years as immigrants, *the still place for the family was a priority.*

What a difference it makes to have this still place.

Growing up, many of us were not quite as fortunate to have that still place at home. But we do have the opportunity, now, to become that still place *for ourselves and for others.*

Stop and feel it calling you.

May 14

Lifeboats Are Standing By

Several years ago, at a time when I felt that my life was on a precarious precipice and there seemed to be no options for me, I had a dream about the precipice.

It was a scary, narrow, dark, and abandoned place.

But as I stood on the ledge, something inside urged me to look up. When I did, I saw a sky brightly illuminated with myriad stars. Then I looked down, way down, to the frightening drop below. There, in the dark ocean beneath the precipice, were hundreds of people bobbing in the water, each with a parachute floating beside them and lifeboats standing by.

I jumped and awoke with new hope.

May 15

The Certain Importance of "Trifles"

I really cannot be certain about much. But I can be certain that if I awoke, if the divine spark is still in my body today, there is something I am here to do, there is someone who needs me, there is a purpose for my existence.

Many days, none of those things are obvious. Life seems to consist of insignificant *stuff.*

Recently, a former boss reminded me that our lives are being observed "out of the corner of the eye" more than we know.

And Andrew Carnegie warned us not to consider anything to be trivial:

"It is upon trifles the best gifts of the gods often hang."

Welcome to Your Future!

Good morning and welcome to your future!

I started saying this with my first waking breath many years ago, as a reminder that, every day, I have the power to choose my future.

Deciding to smile, deciding to hope, deciding to grow as a human being, deciding to say nothing negative all day, deciding to believe the best about others, deciding that all life deserves to be revered, deciding to get my ego out of the way—these are a few of those early morning *futuristic* decisions I have made.

Sometimes it seems that life is just *same ole, same ole.* But I've found that this is never the case.

Today can always be the beginning of a new life and an amazing adventure!

May 17

What Have You Got to Lose?

Cami Walker lost everything—it seemed. She lost her wonderful job, her health, and her hope—all at once. Severely depressed, with no way out of the black hole, she was challenged by a *medicine woman* to get her eyes off herself. She made a twenty-nine-day commitment to give something to someone every day.

Today, Cami Walker's website, *29 Days of Giving*, is making a difference for countless people around the world.

I'm not saying that giving to others is everything, but it is an effective way out of the black hole for many of us.

When we are stuck, when there is nothing we can do to fix our own situation—it may be time to give a hand to someone else.

May 18

Run for Your Life!

I woke up in the middle of the night, my heart racing in panic. In a dream, I had been running desperately, pursued by an abusive captor. It was real enough to remind me of two things.

1. The countless people who are being unjustly pursued, detained, and brutalized by other human beings in this world today
2. How small my challenges are in comparison

When I am lucky enough to live a life in safety, helping those who aren't so lucky might be the thing to do. And it may, also, at times, be the fastest way out of my own life-sucking drama and depression.

Deliver those who are dying and hold back those who are staggering toward the slaughter.

—*Proverbs 24:11*

May 19

Good People Are Standing By

I received an e-mail from someone who had sat in front of me on an airplane and had overheard my conversation with a stranger. She looked me up because she said that the conversation gave her hope.

All around us are good people who just need a little hope: someone, anyone to smile at them and show them a little genuine interest.

Of course, there is that occasional person who might be watching us with sinister motives. But if we are so guarded, protecting ourselves from those few, we will miss the others.

As you grow older, you will discover that you have two hands—one for helping yourself, the other for helping others.

—*Audrey Hepburn*

May 20

Great People Don't Discriminate

It has been said by many that Abraham Lincoln and General Grant were both men who treated *all* people the same, regardless of their position. I have loved reading about the demonstration of this quality in their everyday lives.

This one attribute impresses me more than anything else about a person's character. Often, I have been disappointed to see even my friends pick and choose whom they believe is worthy of their time and attention. Class distinctions, color, race, appearance, any distinctions are poison to an individual—*as they are to a nation.*

Truth: *we all have the same value.*

May 21

The Miracle I Almost Missed

I wrote a book with this title because I believe that this concept is critical to think about every day: *we often miss miracles in our lives because of our biases.*

Many times, we walk right past a person who could be a soul mate, a needed friend, or an important contact. We do this because they do not appear to meet our criteria.

We desperately need to look past our initial impressions of outward appearances to see the person beyond these things.

Try it—and notice how this practice will help you attract more of what you want into your life.

May 22

Hooray for the Uninvited and Unexpected

Many of the good things in my life today have come to me via what I called tragedies at the time. For instance, I have been working in Australia and New Zealand because I lost a lot of money making a film, and I had to pick up contract work from a seminar company—a company that eventually published a book I wrote and asked me to speak in forty-nine states and six foreign countries.

I have discovered that I am generally not a good judge of what is good or bad, so I now refrain from making those calls.

As my good friend Jan reminded me recently by quoting W. C. Fields:

"Never cry over spilt milk, because it may have been poisoned."

May 23

We All Have Our "Stuff"

Gossiping is gossiping is gossiping, whether you are discussing a coworker or a celebrity. It seems to me that we can spend our time and use the airspace so much more efficiently if we quit focusing on how people screw up. We all screw up. We all have our stuff.

Can we just admit that we are sometimes trying to pat ourselves on the back and make ourselves feel better when we talk about other people's craziness?

Maybe we should just work on taking the log out of our own eye first. If we do that, there probably won't be much time left for the other.

Mercy triumphs over judgment.

May 24

No Is a No-No

When my daughter Pammy was eight, she came home after a field trip with a surprise for me. She pulled a flattened chocolate-sprinkle Krispy Kreme donut out of the bottom of her disorderly backpack (that she had generously saved from the store tour) and proudly offered it to me.

I said, "Pammy, I'm *not* eating that!"

She pleaded, so I cautiously took a bite. Later I was unabashedly digging around in the backpack looking for more!

The incident taught me to be slower about saying no. I now try foods without turning up my nose. I try on clothes that I never would have before. I try out ideas before discarding them.

People are very open-minded about new things—as long as they're exactly like the old ones.

—*Charles Kettering*

May 25

Let It Go!

It strikes hardest in the middle of the night: that sudden fear of disaster or failure. Then, the world becomes a frightening place. You can't think of anything that is going right. Every thought seems to bring uncertainty and insecurity with it. Even though most of what we imagine never comes *close* to happening.

This was what I experienced a few nights ago when I was waiting for my daughter to arrive the next day from far away. What if—what if—what if? What a senseless waste of time!

Let it go. Think about whatever it is tomorrow, when you are rested.

Worrying is like a rocking chair, it gives you something to do, but it gets you nowhere.

—*Glenn Turner*

May 26

Your Word Is My Command!

When I decide there is no way out of a dilemma, when I say, "I don't need this right now," I have just given my brain instructions to keep me in darkness, regardless.

My brain buys completely into my valuation of the moment and pulls the subsequent moments into the prison with me.

But if I ask my brain, "How can I handle this right now and make it work?" my brain goes into action, searching for solutions and hope.

I now understand: when I have been locked out of happiness, the essential key was in my own pocket.

May 27

Dormant Seeds of Inspiration?

While checking my luggage in the modern Melbourne, Australia airport, I marveled at the laser, automatically moving over the top of my bag, locating the tag, recording the info, and activating the belt to move it the right direction. Then, I imagined the lifecycle of this technology, from the time it began as a seed of a thought in someone's mind.

All of the modern luxuries, which I often take for granted, became reality because one person was inspired by a *what if* and acted upon it. Someone chose to funnel his or her life force into creating a gift to benefit countless others.

Today, I must ask: if I quieted my mind and released my obsession with "stuff," would I find seeds of inspiration within *me* that, if watered, would grow and nourish the world?

May 28

Airspace Alert!

It's dangerously easy to fall into the habit of moaning, groaning, and talking about how tired I am, or about everything I have to do, or my disappointment with this or that. When I catch myself using the airspace for these topics, I must realize it is an alarm, notifying me that I have taken the *wide path* of mediocrity, am diminishing my own energy and, most likely, am stealing the energy of others in my wake.

Why would I want to waste the airspace and my mind for something like this?

This quote doesn't have to be true of me: "Small things occupy small minds."

May 29

Scary Choices

I was always a big chicken. I wouldn't go out because I was afraid of getting cold. I wouldn't walk up a hill, because I was afraid of falling. I wouldn't play sports because I was afraid of getting hit with the ball. While I was growing up, my brother and sister taunted me, urging me to quit being a crybaby—but I didn't change *until much later in my life.*

When I finally realized that I was missing life because I was afraid of risk and that what I was protecting might not be worth saving, I began to make other choices.

Better late than never.

Two roads diverged in a wood, and I—
I took the one less traveled by,
and that has made all the difference.

—*Robert Frost*

May 30

No Guilt; Just Truth

On Oprah's last show, she made the point that each of us is responsible for the energy we bring to any situation or environment.

This is not only a profound responsibility, but also a profound privilege.

We've got the power! Make a difference with it.

What lies in our power to do, lies in our power not to do.

—*Aristotle*

May 31

Stress Reducer

It was one of those nights full of dreams about not being able to get things done—you know, cars that won't go, the bike that won't pedal, phones that won't dial correctly, a messy house and yard with people coming over, the class I haven't been showing up for the entire semester, etc.

I don't know if it was the KFC right before bed or subconscious fears that I am harboring, but, I woke up in a funk, worried about the day, *until*—

I remembered that my responsibility is simple: be present, love people, be a conduit of positive energy.

Stress—*released*.

Now I am ready.

June

Surrender

Growth demands a temporary surrender of security.

—*Gail Sheehy*

June 1

Perfectionism Released

Today, I woke up feeling the weight of responsibility to be better than yesterday, to make a difference for each of the people I would speak to, and to figure out everything about how I could improve. *I was beat to a bloody pulp before I even got out of bed.*

I had to stop the madness and bring the little I had left to my Creator. I left it there and asked that it be multiplied to fill the needs around me. I acknowledged that the responsibility was not mine. I acknowledged that the Creator was still in charge.

I acknowledged that life is a whole lot bigger than me, and my foremost responsibility is to surrender my illusion of control.

June 2

Hypocritical Panic

While on a speaking trip, I had some major logistical challenges with a seminar. Two hundred and forty people were about to show up, and we were not ready for them. I was running around, crazy, barking orders at people—*trying desperately to recover lost time.*

My conference partner, Debbie, helped me see the irony of what I was doing. I was going to spend the next six hours talking to people about peace when I was not peaceful myself. What a hypocrite!

If I am not at peace while I'm working, I may be efficient, but I am most likely penalizing people around me in the process.

Peace is always the destination. If I get there without it, *I have not arrived.*

June 3

Think Something Good? Say It

Whenever a good thought about someone, anyone, comes to your mind, tell them. Call them. E-mail them. Text them. Write them. They might need that word today, even if you think they already know. *Especially* if you think they already know. Many times they *don't* know—or they may need the message reinforced.

Words like these are valuable gifts that can easily be given without great price or investment. If we *can* make a difference, we should. We can never know the ripple effect of such a small deed.

I have heard many confessions from people who wish they had said those things more when they had the chance.

Seize the opportunity!

(What's the worst that can happen?)

June 4

First Things First, Again

Be generous in prosperity and thankful in adversity.

Be fair in judgment
and guarded in your speech.

Be a lamp to those
who walk in darkness and a home to the stranger.

Be eyes to the blind

and a guiding light to the feet of the erring.

Be a breath of life
to the body of humankind,

a dew to the soil of
the human heart and a fruit upon the tree of humility.

- Baha'i prayer (Braybrooke 2001)

Isn't this prayer nice? Yet, thinking it is nice and doing it are worlds apart. I am keenly aware that I will not be any of these things for others unless I have taken time to get my focus off of my own *stuff.*

I must stop first and feel the creator's love *for me.*

June 5

Call Up the Beautiful

I have seen too many cotton-candy sunrises from my home or while flying high above the earth to ever despair of life again.

I have felt too many refreshing breezes and had too many enlightening conversations with friends and strangers to ever despair of life again.

I have seen too many majestic mountains and endless oceans to ever despair of life again.

I have listened to too many soothing melodies and crashing waterfalls to ever despair of life again.

I must call up these memories and use them as a life-line.

In spite of everything, life is beautiful.

—Etty Hillesum (written on the way to her death in a concentration camp)

June 6

Disconnect Alarm

When things don't make sense, when the world seems too much to bear, when my heart has no motivation, when darkness prevails, when frustrations are more frequent than joys, when I can't think of anything to be grateful for—

These are all alarms, reminding me that I may need to withdraw into the innermost corner of my existence and reconnect to a larger life.

We are never immune from this disconnect.

After many years as an academic and spiritual leader, Dr. Henri Nouwen, world renowned professor, writer, and priest wrote this in his journal:

"Without my one hour a day in prayer and meditation, my life loses its coherency, and I start experiencing my days as a series of random incidents and accidents."

June 7

And Don't Call Back!

I keep the telephone of my mind open to peace, harmony, health, love, and abundance. Then, whenever doubt, anxiety, or fear tries to call me, they keep getting a busy signal—and soon they'll forget my number.

—*Edith Armstrong*

What a powerful visual image about keeping negativity away!

In all practicality, when we decide to tie up the lines with hope, joy, peace, and everything good, we are actually *changing* our "contact info" so that the negative cannot reach us anymore.

Try it and see who blows up your phone.

But first, you must decide whom you want to talk to.

June 8

Drop the Judgment

If today, I met the Pam of ten years ago, I would probably think this about myself: *she is too judgmental; she needs to worry less and learn to be more generous.*

(And I thought I was so together back then!)

On the other hand, since I have been working on not being judgmental, I might just totally ignore her flaws and delight in the person just as she was—*without judgment.*

Ten years in the future, I hope I am even less judgmental, take myself even less seriously, and concentrate even more on the critical things in life: *love and kindness.*

June 9

What I Know About My Anger

In the paradise of Honolulu, I overheard a man yelling angrily at his family in the hotel room next door. The unfortunate situation reminded me of times when I have reacted in anger to people in my own life. For those times in the past (and for the people next door) I am deeply grieved.

For today I fully realize and acknowledge that my anger comes from the threat of some type of loss. To break former patterns that lead to outbursts, I remember that *no one* or *nothing* can take anything away from me that matters.

Anger is a wind which blows out the lamp of the mind.

—*Robert Green Ingersoll*

June 10

"I Never Meet New People"

The antidote to loneliness is a willingness to find connection with everyone.

—*Dalai Lama*

You don't have to be outgoing—just convinced of the value of *all* people. When we survey the world with compassion, everyone becomes *worthy of our attention and interest.*

When your interaction springs from that genuine heart, and you show interest in their lives, *you will find friends wherever you go.*

Here's the problem, though—many of us are being very subtly selective. We have this subconscious measuring stick that kicks people off our radar if they don't measure up. Many of us *talk* compassion but have two categories.

1. interesting people
2. all the others

You may not realize it.

Tune up or turn off your radar today. You'll never be lonely again.

June 11

Gibran on Pain

Your pain is the breaking of the shell that encloses your understanding.

—Khalil Gibran

This is *so* much easier written than experienced!

Yet, I know this: whenever I experience disappointment, pain, or any type of unhappiness, within that experience there is self-revelation. With self-revelation, there is growth. With growth, there is hope. And, with hope, life is worth living.

I used that information *this week* to overcome the blahs brought on by very minor disappointments. My reaction helped me see that I had gotten off track and needed to refresh my focus.

Score!

One thing we do know: Life will give you whatever experience is most helpful for the evolution of your consciousness.

—Eckhart Tolle

June 12

Mrs. Zippy

At a friend's wedding, there was a clown for the kids named Mrs. Zippy. *Really.*

Her name was clever (like Mississippi) but also functional, reminding me to *keep my lips zipped* when I was tempted to tell potentially embarrassing stories about the groom.

I've been known to "get on a roll" in my effort to entertain and inadvertently hurt feelings in the process. So, I told myself, I should practice being *Mrs. Zippy* instead of *Mrs. Zinger*.

It is significant how much more airspace there is when I think before I speak. And it is significant how much more I can find out about others when I am *zipping* rather than *zinging*.

June 13

Gratitude Help

Yesterday, while washing my hands, I stopped thinking about what I had to do next and just noticed *washing my hands:* the foaming soap, the clean, warm water, and the magic movement of my fingers. What a marvel. And I thought about how hard it would be wash my "hands" if I only had one. Such things I take for granted unless I stop and really notice.

After this simple exercise, I was more peaceful. I really felt more connected to sights, sounds, and movement. Life was instantly richer.

Nick Vujicic was born without limbs and has only two little toes on one foot. He has no hands to wash, but wrote a book entitled, *Life without Limits: Inspiration for a Ridiculously Good Life.*

Check it out if you need some gratitude help today.

Slip into Something a Bit More Comfortable

—*And a little less petty.*

I become petty before I realize it sometimes. All of the sudden, I'm complaining about the traffic, the temperature, the food, a messy room, an expression on someone's face or what someone said or *did not say* to me. But when it happens, the result is always the same.

1. A feeling of discontent spreads through my body.
2. I feel joyless.
3. I feel alone and alienated.

When I get these warnings, I must immediately "slip into something more comfortable"— *gratitude.*

By doing so, I step out of the shallow end, into the deep water where the noble are.

He never is alone that is accompanied with noble thoughts.

—*Beaumont and Fletcher*

June 15

Choosing for Me—and You

When I make a commitment to personal transformation, courage, or pursuing my dreams, I am also making a commitment to be a conduit for others' personal transformation, courage, and dreams.

When I decide to give up, to remain stagnant, or discouraged, I have also decided to be a conduit of those states to others as well.

We may think, at times, that no one really cares about what we do. This is never the case. Every action or inaction has a ripple effect out into the world.

Deepak Chopra's advice is to do three things every day.

1. Focus (on your own personal transformation).
2. Serve (do an activity that is not about you).
3. Connect (nurture relationships with others).

June 16

We All Could Use a Good Coach

A coach is someone who tells you what you don't want to hear, who has you see what you don't want to see, so that you can be who you've always known you could be.

—Tom Landry

A good coach once told me that I was the B-word and that was why I had been overlooked for promotion. He said that I could get mad about the perception or I could accept the reality and take some simple steps to change the perception. It worked, and I am grateful now for his courage. At the time, though, I hated his guts!

There are times when we all need some coaching. Good coaches are watching us from the sidelines. When we're ready, they'll talk.

June 17

Just This

For those of us who have a hard time quieting our minds, settling down our pinball brains or not worrying about stuff, there are techniques out there to help us.

It's not enough to tell ourselves to relax, breathe, trust, and rest. We need *more* than that to stop the "OCD machine."

A simple exercise that helps me comes via Deepak Chopra.

There is a short demo video on www.beliefnet.com, but the essence is to breathe in slowly while thinking the word "just" and breathe out slowly with the word "this." Repeat until your head starts to get it—just this moment, just this breath, just this awareness, etc.

A quiet spirit accomplishes much more than our *illusion of control* ever will.

June 18

Who, Me?

Several years ago, when I was a regional manager, my boss, Leslie, gave me a book to read: *How to Be a Better Communicator.* I never read it because I thought that *she* was the one who needed to learn communication skills!

This was one of the biggest mistakes I made in my career. Now I know that, when someone gives me a book, instruction, or a suggestion, there's a good chance I could use the help.

Many character traits that I am working to improve now were pointed out to me earlier in my life by friends, enemies, and family. But I chose to believe that they were just confused, self-righteous, or vindictive, and I didn't change anything.

Wisdom listens without defensiveness or judgment.

June 19

My Father Was Homeless

—Until his second leg amputation put him in an aged-care facility. My sister, brother-in-law, and I were the only attendees at his funeral *until*, toward the end of the service, a gentleman quietly entered. When asked how he knew our dad, he told us the story.

One Sunday, this gentleman decided to get off the couch and volunteer at the local nursing home. He knocked on Louie Gatewood's door and invited him to come listen to gospel singing. Louie cursed at him. The gentleman persevered over a period of several weeks. Louie eventually surrendered, became the gentleman's friend, joined in the singing and, consequently, went from bitter to broken to better.

The gentleman wept when he told us about Louie's transformation.

What a remarkable difference he made for Louie—*and for Louie's family.*

June 20

Selective Listening

I used to be a lot more picky about who I listened to or learned from. Thanks to the influence of some insightful friends who challenged me, I now am *open to learning* from everyone. I may not buy into everything they say, but something they have learned will also be useful to me.

I came about this selective listening honestly. I was afraid of being led astray, down the slippery slope, off the narrow path, so I only read books or listened to audios from people who were in my philosophical camp. Boy, was I missing out!

Those people who were too liberal, too conservative, too intellectual, too simplistic, too old-fashioned, too modern, or too *whatever*—have some *really* good things to say!

Fear strangles truth.

June 21

Surprise Attack of Greed

Be on your guard against every form of greed.

—*Jesus*

I was thinking about the importance of this guidance for life, in general, when I was tested in a very specific way—a security scanner broke at the TSA checkpoint, causing an extended delay. Many people, *including me*, were worried about missing their flights. When we were switched to another line, full-grown adults around me started to argue and bicker about their places in line.

I was close to becoming pushy—but then I thought about greed. I decided that I would miss my flight rather than *miss the point*. It was the right decision.

I shall seek to develop the perfections of generosity, virtue, doing without, wisdom, energy, forbearance, truthfulness, resolution, love, serenity.

—*The Ten Perfections (500 BC), India*

June 22

The Ultimate Irony

I read this excerpt in *Whisper from Your Soul.*

Seek out the person who challenges you the most.
Bless them, send them good thoughts.
You'll be amazed a*t how much they change!*

The other option is to avoid them, stay bitter, be resentful, or say, "They'll never change."

When we will ever learn? Love is the *holy spirit.* Love is the powerful force behind all of creation. Love is the hope we desperately need. Love is the healing we've been looking for.

(Just like Paul, John, George, and Ringo said: "All we need is love.")

June 23

Oops! Did I Say That?

While standing in line to check my luggage, I noticed that a fellow passenger seemed frustrated with the wait. I said, "I've heard they are getting customer service consulting from Qantas, but I guess it hasn't kicked in yet."

Unfortunately, the clerks at the counter overheard my comment, and I pretty much asked for what happened next: they basically ignored me and went out of their way to make sure my service was slower than before.

Seemingly harmless casual complaints like this are not harmless.

Just another embarrassing reminder for me to

1. speak for unintended as well as intended audiences; and
2. weigh the *impact* of my words before I speak them.

I want my words to build, not tear down.

One more time—

People will never forget how you made them feel.

—*Maya Angelou*

June 24

Born This Way

I totally get into this GaGa song because it reminds me to accept people for who they are *and* to accept myself for who I am—without qualifiers.

I was petting our big, fat, black cat the other day, thinking about what a gift she is—just as she is. She didn't have to do anything or accomplish anything to be worthy. She just *is* because she *is*. She has no other purpose really—other than to love and be loved.

It seems that if we judged ourselves this way, we might be much more satisfied with our own lives and, possibly, easier on others.

Maybe we were *all* just born to love and be loved.

June 25

Keep It in Perspective!

Tony Robbins talks about using a "pattern-interrupt" strategy to pull people out of their narrow perspective. For instance, he has been known to throw water in someone's face while they are crying or make someone skydive who is depressed about a permanent spinal cord injury. Really! I know it sounds bizarre and inconsiderate, but the strategy usually works.

I am thankful for those people in my life who have provided "pattern-interrupts" for me, even when I have been fiery mad about it! Keeping my problems, fears, and disappointments in perspective has been key to my mental health.

Life is so much bigger than my stuff. What is more critical is that I remain present, balanced, strong, and courageous.

Someone might need me.

June 26

Raw Fear

Driving down the interstate, out of the blue, I imagined that I was in a bad wreck. Then I started stressing about everything around me: that truck might run me off the road, my car might go over that bridge, I might be paralyzed, or I might die and never be found.

I stopped the craziness by saying to myself,

"So? What am I going to do about it? Pull over, then go home, and sit in my room and never go out again? Protect myself at all costs?"

No! I'm going to live my life to the fullest until whatever happens *happens.*

Fear will steal our lives faster than anything else ever could.

Life happens. Live it.

June 27

Where Would You Rather Be?

The clerk at the grocery store looked completely bored. I told him that he didn't look like he wanted to be there. He said, "I don't."

I said, "So where would you rather be?"

He looked puzzled and said, "I don't really know."

The "ho-hums" or the "undefined blahs" are really an *alarm* that says, "*Stop Immediately! Take stock of the mysterious and incredible things in your life right now!*"

The clerk was a really handsome teenager. He was breathing on his own. He had a job. He had legs, arms, intelligence, sight, hearing, mobility, and a great smile—that he wasn't using.

Recipe for discontent: *take your current circumstances for granted.*

June 28

No Money, No Problem

Listen, everyone who thirsts; even you who have no money. You can come buy wine and milk without money and without cost. Why do you spend your money and your labor for what does not satisfy? Listen carefully to me and your soul will be satisfied.

—*The Prophet Isaiah* (Isaiah 55:1-2)

Several years ago, while I was going into crazy debt to do what I believed in, this passage was my mantra. Today, unbelievably, my six-digit debt is completely paid off, and I am still doing what I love. I didn't end up on the street. The risk was worth it. The path was so very scary at times. The payoff continues to amaze me.

Listen to your soul. It's urging you to risk it all.

June 29

Once You Pass This Line

—You must continue to exit.

This warning is posted in US airports as you leave the boundaries of the secure areas.

I often think of life like this. There are certain things we do that become our futures—whether good or bad. Often, before I have said something in anger or frustration, there was a voice saying,

"Don't! Cool off a minute. Think about it first."

But I said it anyway. And the line I crossed took me into a messy, dark, confusing, and expensive place.

And then there have been times when the voice said,

"Go ahead. Do what you know you should—regardless."

And when I crossed the line, my world improved.

That line—that voice about the line—*tells the future.*

June 30

What's *Your* Word?

If someone asks you, "Hey, what's the word for today?" what will you say?

If you have to think long about an answer, it may mean that you are not living *intentionally*—but *kind of accidentally*.

If you don't choose a word, someone or something will give you one—and you may not like it.

Choose your word. Choose your mood. Choose your path.

Not choosing is a choice. You've got the power (to choose what your life will be) *if you want it!*

July

Awareness

*I think that growth and spiritual awareness come in slow increments.
Sometimes you don't know it is happening.*

—*Mariel Hemingway*

July 1

Don't Miss the "Angels"

Two smiling, helpful "angels" came into my path last night, but I almost missed them. I would have missed seeing them because I had been bombarded with frustrating circumstances, and I thought I had the right to be irritated.

If I had given in to the foul mood, I would not have even noticed these two kind beings who brightened up my world. I also would not have noticed the clear, beautiful evening. And, when I finally arrived at home, I would have not noticed when I brought my foul mood into the lives of my family.

Good reminder.

I weave a silence on my lips
I weave a silence into my mind
I weave a silence within my heart

—An old Celtic prayer

July 2

Open the Johari Window

In 1955, two guys named Joe and Harry developed a model called the *Johari Window* to demonstrate the multiple facets of our own self-awareness.

The model includes four quadrants, or "windows."

Open: Things about me that I know *and* others know

Blind: Things about me that others know *but* I don't

Hidden: Things about me that I know *but* I do not reveal to others

Unknown: Things about me that are only known by my subconscious *and* by no one else

I mentioned the Johari Window in a class, making a point about blind spots in our lives. A woman in the class said she didn't have any blind spots. *Her coworkers quickly changed her mind.*

Enlarging the "open" quadrant of this model yields a more fulfilling life.

July 3

It Runs in the Family

Toward the end of my mother's life, when she struggled with dementia, I took her to a bar in Midland, Texas. The circumstances were stressful, and she had been impatient and a bit cantankerous.

"What are we doing here, anyway?" she asked.

"We're here to visit Angela," I replied.

"Who is Angela?"

"She's your youngest daughter."

"How many children do I have?"

"Five: Linda; Steve; me; Ronnie, who died several years ago; and Angela who is here, dying of cancer."

To which my mother responded, "My God, it runs in the family."

A profound observation.

Unfortunately, it does run in the family. None of us get out alive. So today I'm going to look my mortality in the face and live this moment as if it's my last.

July 4

Happy Fourth, *but,* I Hate Your Guts

Thomas Jefferson and John Adams were bitter political rivals who reconciled in their later years (thanks to the efforts of a friend who saw the benefit of their friendship to each other and to the country).

Their friendship became a remarkable collaboration, and, on July 4th, 1826, on the fiftieth anniversary of the signing of the Declaration of Independence, the two men both died, within hours of each other. Unaware that his friend had died hours earlier, Adams's last spoken words were, "Jefferson still survives."

I love this story because of its reminder that true independence comes when we release resentment, judgment, and hatred—when we allow all to live and thrive in our world.

As Jefferson and Adams, we may find there was *always* room in the world for everyone.

July 5

Looking Back on the American Holiday

Frederick Douglas, a slave who became a great public speaker for the cause of liberation, often commented on the way slaves felt while observing Americans celebrate their independence. The holiday seemed cruel and hypocritical to those who had no independence.

It is important for us to remember that.

The two calls to action for me are:

1. Fight for freedom all over the world, wherever I have the power to do so.
2. Don't be a hypocrite. Respect *all* people and their need for life, liberty, and the pursuit of happiness.

Happy fifth of July!

July 6

Duh! I Coulda Had a V8!

In Florence Scovel Shinn's book, *The Game of Life and How to Play It,* she gives the three rules for playing.

1. Fearless Faith—We'll either trust in goodness or trust in evil. Choose to trust the good the Universe wants to give.
2. Nonresistance—*All* is well and *all* happens for a reason.
3. Love—Make sure the energy we bring to life is positive, forgiving, and free of resentment.

Looking back on my life, I now see that I fretted, despaired, blamed, and complained way too much. But *I'm making up for lost time today!*

So often times it happens that we live our lives in chains. And we never even know we have the key.

—The Eagles, "Already Gone"

July 7

"I Will Return"

Three years ago, a thriving willow tree in our backyard did not exist. A violent storm had pulled it completely out of the ground. The tree was cut into pieces and carried away, except for the stump, which was put back into the hole.

We named the tree *Wilson* because, later that year, the stump sprouted leaves and resembled the soccer ball with "hair" in the movie *Castaway*.

Today, Wilson is fuller and healthier than the other willow in our backyard that survived the storm, untouched.

Wilson gives me hope. Wilson reminds me to never despair of the storms or the damage that comes from them.

Strength and hope arrive in very strange packages.

July 8

The Sting of Mortality

Recently, a gut-wrenching tragedy occurred at a Texas Rangers baseball game when a father-son outing ended in horror. The father, attempting to catch a fly-ball for his son, fell to his death while his son watched.

How do we explain and live with the pain of such abrupt, nonsensical abortion of life?

Countless people suffer every day with similar pain. They've watched individuals they love suffer and die, some from tragic accidents for which they feel responsible, some from the carelessness of others, some from malevolent forces against which they felt powerless.

The shock. The confusion. The guilt. The anger. The loneliness.

No easy answers.

Trust. Hope. Wait for the rest of the story.

July 9

Apologize to Flies?

I heard my husband, Bernie, apologizing to a fly as he whacked it to its noble death in our kitchen. It made me smile because this apologizing-to-bugs-thing is also my habit. (How on earth did we ever find each other?)

Of course, I know the habit is weird—even though its source is reverence for all living things.

But the ironic thing is this: it is much easier to care for and honor animals than it is to honor and respect a human being who irritates us in traffic, takes our parking space, or runs for political office.

A true reverence for life includes family members who have hurt us, politicians in the other party, people of rival nations, and strangers in all socio-economic brackets.

All deserve our respect.

July 10

The Balancing Act of Awareness

Awareness requires a rupture with the world we take for granted; then old categories of experience are called into question and revised.

—*Shoshana Zuboff (American Educator)*

I like the word "rupture" that Zuboff uses here because it accurately reflects the violence of awareness. When I first made a commitment to a higher level of awareness, my foundations crumbled around me; the world was not as tidy and easily defined as I had formerly imagined, and I was no longer separate from anyone else. Everyone mattered.

Then, because I cared more, I had to fight off despair over the depth of pain and suffering in the world.

The balance I found was to first approach the world with joy. There I received the energy needed to sustain compassion.

July 11

"I See You"

Virtue begins when he dedicates himself actively to the job of gratitude.

—*Ruth Benedict*

Yesterday, I had to ask for help from someone I had just met.

I noticed that she was so much more energetic about helping me after I had praised her for the excellent work she was already doing and the good things I had observed in her area of responsibility.

I wasn't schmoozing. I was merely making an effort not to take anyone or anything *for granted*.

It is so easy to make important people in our lives feel better and more interested in us.

- Show them that we are not taking them for granted.
- Show them that we have already taken time to really see them.

July 12

Whining, Clawing, or Grabbing

If something takes whining, clawing, or grabbing to get it, it may not be worth getting.

In my own experience, when I've tainted the prize with greed, the prize steals my soul and, later, becomes a burden to me.

In the movie *The Other Boleyn Girl,* Anne desperately wants to be queen. She claws and pushes her way in front of her sister, Mary— only to get the same brutal treatment from another woman shortly thereafter.

What we sow, we will always reap.

When I think I desperately need something, the first step is to realize that, if it *really* is mine. by divine right, no one or nothing can keep it from me or take it away from me. I never have to beg, cheat, lie, steal, or worry to get or keep it.

It will come to me—*accompanied by joy.*

July 13

Intuition Trumps Decorum

A few years ago, while I was working in Orange, New South Wales, I caught sight of a woman in a downtown cafe, sitting alone, looking immensely depressed. Something prodded me to speak to her, but for fear of violating "cultural decorum," I didn't.

Her image has haunted me for three years.

The *Year of Kindness Blog* told a similar story about the author, who was also prodded to speak to a woman sitting alone in a shopping mall. She obeyed her intuition, in spite of the decorum argument, and struck up a conversation with the woman. The woman, initially slow to respond, in the end, said, "Thank you for talking to me. No one has shown any interest in me for such a long time."

Poignant message.

July 14

Two Reasons Why We Lose

Oh, yes, the rest of the story of Anne Boleyn: she eventually lost her head in the greed game.

We definitely want to avoid those stakes— and all the other negative repercussions of improperly motivated actions.

That doesn't mean that we should become passive about our goals and needs but, instead, we should enjoy a state of relaxed expectancy about them.

This is the secure place where we avoid the two primary catalysts of greed, which are:

1. the *fear of loss*
2. the *failure to appreciate and accept* what we already have

If you want to "keep your head," get these two toxic items off the menu now!

Start by

1. Acknowledging that your happiness does not depend on anything or anyone *except you*; and
2. Taking *nothing* for granted—*notice* and *delight* in everyone and everything.

Where Am I Going to Get Pennies and Quarters?

Several years ago, while managing a restaurant, I found myself drastically short-staffed. Functioning as the boss, the hostess, and the cashier, with a long line of people waiting to be seated and a long line of angry people waiting to pay at the register, I ran completely out of change. I had *no one* to help, so I prayed, "God, will you please get me pennies and quarters?"

The very next customer threw down rolls of pennies and quarters, saying,

"I sure hope you don't mind if I pay with these."

I told the story at home that evening, and my insightful young son, Hudson, impressed with my quick prayer results, said, "Wow, Mom! Next time ask for twenty-dollar bills!"

Ask and it shall be given ...

July 16

Do Everything Like it Matters

Scrubbing my closets, tubs, and floors for the family who had just purchased our home, I resisted the urge to cut corners and, instead, cleaned it the way I would want it done for myself.

How much simpler things would have been earlier in life if I had always done everything (school, work, chores, errands, etc.) with this much conscientiousness!

I read about a woman who, for over thirty years, in the basement of St. Jude's Hospital, has packed sterilized surgical instruments for the next day's procedures. While working, she thinks about how much the instruments will mean to the patient's family, and she prays for every person who is to be operated upon. As a result, her job becomes more critical and is never tedious for her.

Everything does matter.

July 17

I Spy

Sometimes, we get so caught up in making our own way through the world that we fail to see the people on every side of us who are immersed in the same struggle.

Yesterday, at the post office, I noticed something about the simple courtesy of holding a door open for someone: it can shake us free of *our own agenda* for a few seconds.

Simple courtesies (done with heart) say, *"I see others' burdens to be just as important as my own."*

When I do, I am happier. And I am more patient in traffic and kinder in the grocery store.

It's not what you look at that matters, it's what you see.

—*Thoreau*

See more today.

July 18

Know Your Bore-Score

We all know boring people: people who talk too much, people who talk about the same things over and over, people who complain all the time, people who don't ever talk, and people who never show interest in anyone except themselves.

Today, I will do my part in the quest to stop *global boring* by

- showing interest in the challenges others are facing;
- not talking about predictable things like how hot it is, how bad politicians are, or how tired I am; and
- saying things that will motivate, encourage, and uplift people.

I will work on achieving a lower bore-score.

How refreshing it is when we use the airspace positively and thoughtfully—and, how desperately we all need friends who will do that today!

July 19

Never Be Bored Again

Have you ever been in a social setting where there is no one interesting to engage in conversation—where your soul retreats and simply waits for it to be over?

People who are a*ware, appreciative, available, and accountable* (really *seeing* people around them, instead of focusing on their own agendas, and taking responsibility for adding value) will never be bored. These people (extroverts *or* introverts*)* find light and bring it with them.

On the other hand, *anxiety, anger, apathy, and arrogance* will guarantee a boring event. While in these states, we bring the "gray" with us.

July 20

The Vulnerable Psychic

When I was thirteen, I went down a hill on my bicycle, spun out on gravel, and tore up my knee. I thought I was psychic because I knew I was going to wreck before starting down the hill.

I told everyone about it as proof that I could predict the future!

Now, I believe it was my lack of confidence that caused the wreck.

But isn't it true? I can predict the future! We all can. Our brain takes orders from our words and thoughts.

Think twice before you speak, because your words will plant the seed of either success or failure in the mind of another.

—*Napoleon Hill*

July 21

The Geography of Sadness

I wrote this a few years ago. This depth of sorrow is, thankfully, now only a vague memory. I share it here to remind myself and others that life will find us again if we wait for it.

Mercy to those who suffer today—

Sorrow has swallowed me
And spit me out
Onto the shore of my life
Barely breathing, I die the death of desertion
I know life is somewhere out there but cannot lift my head from this wet sand
The ocean is only this wave that approaches, closer and closer
Then engulfs, subsides, and comes again
Motionless, I submit with burning eyes, my flesh a leaden weight
That cannot rise
To receive the gifts of the sea
Just beyond the horizon

July 22

Practical Advice for Dealing with Misfits

John Elder Robison's book *Be Different*, Daniel Tammet's *Born on a Blue Day*, and Temple Grandin's story reminds me never to write off anyone or label them as unimportant because they are not *normal, predictable,* or *like me.*

The injustice we do ourselves and others when we devalue or undervalue someone based on outward conformity to arbitrary standards or because we don't understand them, is immeasurable.

I will make a commitment today to admire and delight in everyone without judgment. Will you do so, too? One thing this means is that we will listen more carefully to what we think about people and be aware of who we criticize.

(And there is a wonderful side effect to this level of self-awareness: we may, as a result, go easier on *the misfit* within ourselves.)

July 23

She Was So Rude!

Yesterday, I thought this about a women who seemed unfriendly after an attempt to exchange pleasantries with her. But I stopped short of the premature judgment and said to myself,

Really? Are you sure? Or is it possible that her reaction was related to something far deeper? Maybe she has Asperger's syndrome. Maybe she was scared or just had indigestion. Maybe she is very different from me in personality, upbringing, or culture."

Realizing that I don't know enough about someone to judge their motives has been an important part of growing up for me.

What a different world it would be if we all gave each other just a little more slack—allowing others the benefit of a doubt—as we desire it for ourselves.

July 25

There Is an Amazing Something
Waiting in the Wings

I've very reluctantly, and with much difficulty, found this to be true: nothing is ever lost or taken away from us that doesn't create a space for something else that we will (most certainly) need later.

Looking back, I see countless wasted days in pain, depression, and worry over what I feared I could never regain, cursing fate, or reliving events over and over in a desperate attempt to recover the "spilled milk" of my errors or loss.

I'm now convinced that by blessing the loss with faith and hope, as with rain on a new seedling, I will, a little later, find something, *an amazing something*, has filled the spot which was once barren.

Weeping may last for the night, but joy comes in the morning.

—Psalm 30

July 26

Hey, You Messed Up My Picture!

I usually have an all-will-work-out-for-good attitude *until* I am forced to wait longer than I anticipated.

When I don't get an immediate fix, see the way out of the darkness, or have proof of help coming around the bend, I despair.

"How dare God mess with my happiness like this? I had a picture of how my life should be. Now look at it! It's completely wrecked!"

But if I had only waited just a little bit longer, I may have gained a certain poise that would have benefited me in years to come.

I may have grown stronger in mind, spirit, and body. I may have seen the light of dawn—*and gotten a few less wrinkles on my face.*

July 27

Magic Phrases

Helping my nephew turn a difficult boss-relationship around, Ken Bradford, founder of *The Leader's Course*, used Chick Fil'A's policy of saying, "It's my pleasure," in response to customer requests.

It's my pleasure, I'd love to, I'll be happy to, I'm honored that you asked, etc. are magic phrases when it comes to making a very quick difference in the dynamic of any relationship.

These phrases take our attitude from *hum-drum* to *wow!*

Take the challenge this week, at home, at work, anywhere you have difficult people in your life. Instead of rolling your eyes, arguing, resisting, or resenting their requests or criticisms, say instead,

"I'd love to," or "Thank you, I'm honored that you asked."

Change always starts with us.

July 28

Instant Character Therapy

When I was a freshman at the University of Oklahoma, I developed a habit. But this habit changed my life *for the better.*

In a lecture someone, challenged me to consciously take charge of my thoughts. The first day I tried it was a virtual slap in the face. Previously, I was unaware my thoughts needed adjusting. I had no idea they were so utterly self-centered and screwed-up.

Now, decades later, I seldom waste my time being critical or judgmental of others but automatically offer a blessing or prayer of help when I encounter (or even see or hear of) someone cruel, undisciplined, arrogant, etc.

As a result, I pray for others continuously and keep my ego from calling the shots.

July 29

A Room with a View

I've noticed when I'm traveling in other countries that people seldom *fully appreciate* where they live. So, I decided that, when I am at home, I will look out my window every day and pretend that I am on vacation. I open the blinds and pretend it's the first time I've ever seen the view from my window. Wow! What a nice place!

There is never a morning that my heart doesn't beat faster with joy to see the lovely sun shining on the lawn, ominous clouds in the sky, a million leaves on the old tree, or the birds sitting on the fence. I try to soak it all in—as if *I may never pass this way again.*

July 30

Never Underestimate Any
Moment, Any Encounter

I listened to the pilot sitting beside me spout negativity for hours. When he asked what I was thinking, I suggested a book for him to read.

He jumped up and retrieved the *very book* from his flight bag. It had been recommended to him two weeks earlier by another woman on another plane.

He gave me her business card. She lived in my city. I called her. We became friends. She suggested *The Alchemist*. That book helped me understand my life and filled me with hope. That book led to more books and better thoughts about my life and our friendship led to more hope for both of us.

All moments are fertile soil.

It takes half your life before you discover life is a do-it-yourself project.

—*Napoleon Hill*

July 31

How Dare We?

When I listen to the worries of my nephew, I hear myself. His biggest frustration is that people think he is stupid. I also spent years of my life feeling ashamed about things I was born with: my body, crazy parents, no money, no talents, etc.

But one day I woke up, laughed at myself, *accepted it all as good,* and began using *all of it* to make a difference. My nephew's IQ *is* lower than normal, but what we were born with is *not our problem!*

How dare we decide our own worth or someone else's worth based on something over which we had no control?

August

Finding Peace

*Every goal, every action, every thought, every feeling one experiences,
whether it be consciously or unconsciously known, is an attempt to
increase one's level of peace of mind.*

—*Sydney Madwed*

August 1

Live the Questions

Have patience with everything unresolved in your heart
and try to love the questions themselves—
Don't search for the answers,
they could not be given to you now,
because you would not be able to live them.
And the point is, to live everything.
Live the questions now.
Perhaps then, someday in the future,
you will gradually, without even noticing it,
live your way into the answer.

—Rainer Maria Rilke (Braybrooke 2001)

Whatever our challenges today, it will serve us well to live the questions: to give ourselves to everything, savoring, noticing, and participating. If we get caught up in our own drama, we miss so much life that is within our grasp this moment.

See it, feel it, and drink it in. Joy will come.

August 2

With Eyes Wide Open

I slept and dreamt that life was joy. I awoke and saw that life was service. I acted and behold, service was joy.

—Tagore

I'm not saying that service can fix everything, but I have seen enough evidence that suggests that, when our scope is broadened to encompass the needs of others, we benefit.

Last week, I had the opportunity to volunteer in a camp for children with developmental delays. Most of the full-time counselors were eighteen to twenty-one years old. Their work was intense, but their joy was even more so.

If you don't know where to serve, try this: run your errands, but with eyes wide open to see the needs of others. Pass out kindness, attention, prayers, and maybe even a little money.

Just see if peace is out there looking for you.

August 3

Look the World Straight in the Eye

Never bend your head. Always hold it high. Look the world straight in the eye.

—Helen Keller

Sure, the world is screwed up. Throughout history, there have been innumerable, unspeakable injustices done, brutal murders and genocides of innocent people, callous bullying by those in places of power, and painfully destructive displays of hatred and hostility. *But there have also always been people who have lived lives of light in the darkest dark.*

Looking the world *straight in the eye,* as Keller recommends, doesn't mean wasting our time fretting about, murmuring against, or fearing the *bad people.* It also doesn't mean pretending that the entire world is wonderful.

It means rising above it all as our heroes have shown us we can.

Even the blind can see that.

August 4

What Power of Positive Thinking?

The power of positive thinking, rejoice always, in everything give thanks, look at the bright side, the law of attraction, etc. We've heard these messages over and over again from preachers, teachers, motivational speakers, relatives, friends, books, and movies, *ad infinitum*.

I thought I *got it*, but really didn't. I didn't get it because, *in between my positive thoughts,* I was busy hating myself, fretting, criticizing others, or moaning about my pathetic circumstances. My friend Jean Osborne pointed this out to me once (from the wheelchair she had been using for twenty years) but I thought she didn't understand and was being insensitive and cruel to me.

So I didn't change anything.

And peace didn't come until I *heard* her.

August 5

It Is a Good Day!

As much as I tried to utilize all the "positive energy" approaches to life, the power of positive thinking only became powerful for me when I quit *judging* the moment and started *living* in the moment—completely.

What my friend Jean Osborne had been trying to tell me was to "let it go and live." She knew. Life for her didn't depend on her circumstances. My journal revealed, instead, an up-and-down, up-and-down existence. But not anymore.

Today, I bring my *whole self* to the moment, *whatever* the moment is; I completely surrender to the experience without judgment. I don't have to hope for a good day. *It is a good day!*

No Worries; No Drama

I'm not offended by all the dumb blonde jokes because I know I'm not dumb—and I also know that I'm not blonde.

—Dolly Parton

I love this quote because it reminds me of two very important truths.

1. If I get prickly when someone criticizes me, it may be because I do have issues that I am trying to hide or am afraid to confront.
2. If I get prickly when someone criticizes me, it may be because I am taking myself too seriously.

Like Dolly, if I know I am not dumb, I have absolutely nothing to worry about. If I am dumb, I'll own it, and then focus on something else that *is* my strength.

No worries. No drama. Thanks for the feedback.

August 7

Small Thing; Big Difference

In my early twenties, I read a biography of George Mueller and have never forgotten the account of himself as a brokenhearted young boy, working away from home. At a very low point in his life, a kind gentleman crossed his path and took the time to stop and speak kindly to him as a peer and then left fifty cents in George's hand. With that small deed, the man made a lifelong impression on George Mueller and, consequently, the futures of many, many others.

It only takes a little to make a big difference for someone.

Today, there will be people in our paths who desperately need someone to *see* them.

Let no one come to you without leaving better.

—*Mother Teresa*

August 8

If You Build It, They Will Come

Be thine own palace, or the world's thy jail.

—*John Donne*

If we can simply think one positive thought, if we will choose to reject the recurring negative feeling, if we can fake a smile, if we can refuse to hate, if we decide *not* to make that critical comment, if we do small acts of kindness, if we can utter prayers instead of judgments, if we give the benefit of a doubt, then, we will commence the building of our palace.

Keep doing these small acts, and the electricity, gardens, furniture, and ballrooms will be added.

Make your life about these things, and people will flock to the *parties you throw* there.

The jail will become a very vague memory.

August 9

Take the Joystick Back!

Either you run the day or the day runs you.

—*Jim Rohn*

All the sages say it. Do you believe it? Do you believe you have a choice or that you are a victim? Do you ever say at the end of the day, "I had a terrible day?"

If you have, you may be letting the day run you.

I can't remember the last time I said or thought that phrase. I can remember saying I had a challenging day, but cannot remember the last time I gave up the joystick of my life to someone or something else.

I'm not saying that everything always goes well. I am saying we have the power to call it joy—or call it pain.

Take control. *It belongs to you!*

August 10

What's on the Menu?

Every time you get angry, you poison your own system.
Expect problems and eat them for breakfast.

—*Alfred A. Montapert*

Just try this today: imagine yourself gobbling down your problems and licking your plate clean of them. Maybe it wasn't what you ordered, but they made it to your table anyway. So, instead of letting them get the better of you, you'll make a savory meal of them.

Ready?

Spread the napkin on your lap. Pick up your knife and fork. Now, carve them up into tiny bite-size pieces. Then, wash them down with some champagne to celebrate your victory.

Go ahead and indulge—even though it's only breakfast!

Sure tastes better than poison.

August 11

Work or Play—It's All Okay!

I simply do not distinguish between work and play.
To pay attention, this is our endless and proper work.

—Mary Oliver, poet and philosopher

The more I learn to really live, the more I find Mary Oliver's words in both of these statements to be true.

When I really pay attention to everything in the moment, work becomes play: stimulating, interesting, engaging, life-giving.

I have also noticed while playing golf, tennis, or even solitaire, that when I quit really paying attention to everything in the moment, play becomes work: frustrating, confounding, disappointing, and a burden.

I am guaranteed a good time—whatever I am doing—if I am completely and totally alert and present right now.

Let the fun begin!

August 12

Married to What?

When it's over, I want to say: all my life I was a bride married to amazement. I was the bridegroom, taking the world into my arms.

—*Mary Oliver*

Unfortunately, for the first four decades of my life, I cannot say this. I was more like a bride married to struggle, a fighter in the ring, fighting my partner as if he was my opponent every day, instead of embracing him as he asked.

It took me a long time to realize that the world was my partner, not my opponent. It took me a long time to cease from the struggle and rest—even though the sages, poets, preachers, philosophers, singers, artists, and writers all told me to.

But—again—I'm making up for lost time. It's never too late!

August 13

Plato's Recommendations

Plato taught that, in order to be a complete person, one must concentrate on three areas of harmony and virtue:

- *Our appetites must be controlled so they do not control us.*
- *Our reason must aspire to wisdom.*
- *Our will must aspire to courage.*

Easier said than done.

Since I am, often, by nature, an obsessive, narcissistic, wimpy chicken, I've had major trouble with all of these. I had to find considerable help outside myself.

So, at nineteen, I made the commitment to spend time every day reading, praying, and meditating.I read countless biographies of courageous people and hung out with people like you.

For many years, I fasted weekly.

Radical investment.

Dividends were not often immediate, but when they did come, they were exponential.

Plato was a smart dude.

August 14

Dropping the *If*

Today will be a good day. Today *is* a good day. I've already decided.

Come what may, this is the day appointed for me, and I have been given all the resources to manage it. I have accepted my power to make it good, to find the good, to bless it as it comes, to completely experience it, and allow my "spiritual muscles" to be stretched, nourished, and enlarged by *all* that comes.

As opposed to saying, today will be a good day *if* certain things occur or don't occur.

I am dropping the *if*.

Attitudes are the forerunners of conditions.

—*Charles Edwards*

August 15

I Have *No* Tale of Woe

In the book and movie *Jane Eyre,* Mr. Rochester asks Jane (with cynicism) for her tale of woe. Jane, who possessed a tortuous past, says she has none. Many years earlier, she had determined to overcome that past and to be thankful for all she had endured.

We all have a tale of woe. Jane Eyre is a literary model for dealing with our pain, disappointment, rejection, and bitterness. Like Jane, when we deal graciously with these things, our energy changes and we will begin to draw healing and good into our lives.

When our hearts are open, we will hear this message from spiritual teachers, from literature, from philosophy, from nature, and from the entire universe.

They can't all be wrong.

August 16

Formula for Peace

$C/a = D$ *(Circumstances over Attitude equals Discontent)*

$A/c = P$ (Attitude over Circumstances equals Peace)

Every day.

Choose your attitude early and often.

August 17

Laugh Yourself Well

Hearty laughter is a good way to jog internally without having to go outdoors.

—Norman Cousins

Norman Cousins chronicles the validity of this quote and the adage of laughter being the best medicine in *Anatomy of an Illness*.

He had recovered from a very serious illness by checking out of the hospital and into thirty days of Groucho Marx and *The Three Stooges*. He literally laughed himself to health!

My mother led a pretty tragic life and there were many times when our lives were anything but funny, but jokes were always on the menu.

Whatever you do today—laugh! Don't take yourself so seriously. It will give your psyche the exercise it needs to get you back where you belong.

August 18

Today I Say, *Bull!*

For many years, I felt invisible, insignificant, and unimportant. To that thinking, this morning, I say, *"Bull!"*

Today I will not wait for someone to affirm my worth.

Today I will own my place in the world!

Today I will live, move, and speak with the confidence that I am valuable and created for a purpose!

And, in order for this behavior not to be obnoxious to others, I will remember this:

Every single human being has the same inestimable worth and purpose. Not one of them is merely a prop in my world. All have been stamped with the Infinite and the Divine, and all deserve to be treated in that manner—*regardless of how they see me.*

No Enemies—Just Teachers

Eckhart Tolle tells the story of a peaceful monk who was accused by a young girl of fathering her unborn child. Instead of defending himself, he took the child after it was born and raised it, bearing the shame peacefully. Later in life, after the woman owned the lie, the monk was not bitter; rather, he was thankful for the experience; the child had been given a good home and he, the joy of raising a son.

I will remember this story on the days I feel like I have sacrificed to do the right thing but feel unappreciated, misinterpreted, or rejected. I will learn from the experience and remember that I have no enemies—only teachers.

All serve us somehow. Nothing has to steal our joy.

August 20

Solemn Day

Life is both sad and solemn. We are let into a wonderful world, we meet one another here, greet each other — and wander together for a brief moment. Then we lose each other and disappear as suddenly and unreasonably as we arrived.

—Jostein Gaarder (from Sophie's World)

Beautifully said.

I will keep this in mind today when I am tempted to take my challenges or myself too seriously.

Here's to a great day.

May we wander together—*and wonder together*—until we meet again.

August 21

"Face" Your Day

I caught my reflection in the computer screen while blogging the other day: a furrowed brow, pursed lips, clenched teeth. Wow! Since then, I've made a conscious effort while I think and work to smile more and relax more.

I want my "default" face to be a face of joy and pleasure, not a face of "me-against-the-world."

Ever notice that face on crotchety old people? Let's stop that train now.

Here's to a day of joy and optimism!

August 22

Life without Worry

I found myself worrying this week about things I could not change—other people, a sick pet, time, war, brutality, etc. I even woke up once last night with the free-floating, universal, pit-in-the-stomach variety of anxiety.

It went away immediately, though, when I thought of the worst possible things that happen to people *and* how worrying never stops any of those things, but belief, conviction, passion, joy, and love have stopped them or, at least, made them more bearable and redemptive.

Daniel was thrown into a den with hungry lions, but they didn't eat him. When Dietrich Bonhoeffer was hung for conspiring against Hitler, he died in complete peace. We can believe the countless stories like this or—we can worry.

August 23

Emily Solves the Mystery

If I can stop one heart from breaking
I shall not live in vain;
If I can ease one life the aching,
Or cool one pain,
or help a fainting robin unto his nest again,
I shall not live in vain.

—*Emily Dickenson* (Dickenson 1924)

So here's the drill:

- Replace a negative thought with a positive one.
- Replace malice with a small kindness.
- Replace despair with a little hope.
- Remember to love that difficult person instead of hate them.
- Smile instead of frown.

It's that easy to solve the mystery.

Thanks, Emily.

August 24

Yield to the Urge to Be You

All that writers can do is keep trying to say what is deepest in their hearts.

—Lloyd Alexander

When I start feeling like my work is meaningless, this quote encourages me to just keep the conduit of words open, to keep yielding to the urge to create.

I've been writing for many years, but it wasn't until recently that I was courageous enough to say, *I am a writer.*

I now know that I write because it is who I am.

I hope you will, today, yield to the urge to be completely and totally *You.*

I revere this page
This pen
This time to write
To bend
My feelings into words
Like light
Into color

August 25

I Want to Be Like Mark Twain

A man's character may be learned from the adjectives which he habitually uses in conversation.

Drag your thoughts away from your troubles—by the ears, by the heels, or any other way you can manage it.

—Mark Twain

These are two separate quotes but go together to make quite a point.

None of us enjoys being around someone who is a perpetual complainer, but many of us complain *subtly* much more than we realize. Listen to your *adjectives* today when you comment on your challenges, weather, politicians, coworkers, bosses, your relatives, and traffic.

Then, *drag your thoughts away from your problems* and into places that bring smiles, peace, and *even* laughter.

This skill made Mark Twain forever adored!

And we can access that skill *today.*

August 26

Just a Little Rain Will Do Miracles

A single gentle rain makes the grass many shades greener. So our prospects brighten on the influx of better thoughts.

—Thoreau

This morning, after I took a bath and put on clean clothes, I noticed how refreshed my body felt. It struck me how my spirit longs for that type of refreshment as well.

This Thoreau quote is one of my favorites because it reminds me how quickly things change with just a little refreshment. All of nature sings this simple secret.

Take time to refresh your spirit today. Immerse it in a pool of hopeful thoughts, positive words, and wisdom from the sages all around you.

Your hope, help, and refreshment are much closer than you realized.

Let your thoughts provide the rain.

August 27

No More Guilt

I used to beat myself up over all the mistakes I've made, periodically falling into the black hole of self-hatred, wishing I hadn't done *something so stupid,* or that I wasn't *such a total loser,* etc.

Now, in those lucid moments when I see myself from another angle that challenges the image I have of myself as loving, honest, or insightful, I literally rejoice: "Yes! And God loves me anyway! God has always known and loved me for who I am: flaws and all. Yea! I'm human, and that's okay!"

This love motivates me so much more than guilt ever could.

August 28

Fear *Never* Serves Me Well

I used to "tactfully" nag my son about going to college every time I saw him. I justified this nagging because I loved and wanted the best for my son. But in actuality, that behavior was motivated by fear. I was worried and afraid that he was going to waste his fine mind and fail to utilize his gifts.

Fear and worry cannot accomplish what love intends. Instead, fear and worry send images of doom and gloom out into the universe. And—

Thoughts become things.

The *best* I can do for those I love is to banish fear and see images of their happiness and success, in whatever form it comes to them.

There is no fear in love. Perfect love casts out fear.

—*St. John*

August 29

Escape to Your Destiny!

If you do not feel yourself growing in your work and your life broadening and deepening, if your task is not a perpetual tonic to you, you have not found your place.

—*Orison Swett Marden*

The sad thing about this quote is that, for many years, I knew I had not found my place, but I felt that it was impossible to do so. In actuality, *I was merely averse to risk taking.* I didn't know that it was okay to fail. I didn't understand the art of possibility.

If I had it to do over again, every single time I thought, *"This is who I am,"* or, *"This is what I do effortlessly,"* I would ask, "What's my next step to utilize and develop this strength?"

And I would take that step.

August 30

Peace Mentors

If we have no peace, it is because we have forgotten that we belong to each other.

—*Mother Teresa*

She's not just talking about the global variety either.

This quote is for *anyone* who, today, may be anxious, troubled, vengeful, or angry.

Some helpful and practical tenants of Mother Teresa's *peaceful, strong* life:

- My peace is closely tied to practical love (acts of kindness).
- My peace is unsustainable until I learn when someone else loses, so do I.
- My peace comes when I let go of the fear that someone else will get my "stuff."
- I am peaceful when I am concerned not just about my world, but also about the dignity of others *outside my borders.*

Got peace?

Peace mentors are standing by.

August 31

Counterpoint

About yesterday's peace message—

Doing acts of kindness for others will not necessarily bring peace. Some of us have been serving and serving and still have no peace.

Two things must happen *first:*

1. You must do an act of kindness *for yourself* by quietly affirming your own worthiness (apart from what you do).
2. You must make sure *no strings are attached* to your gifts (expect *nothing* in return from anyone).

But, just to be clear, that doesn't mean you should wait indefinitely before you do something kind.

Often, ready or not, we just need to jump-start our peace by doing something outside our normal routine.

So, when all else fails, set sail.

Go surprise the world with joy!

September

The School of Life

*I had a terrible education. I attended a school
for emotionally disturbed teachers.*

—*Woody Allen*

How Many Times Do I Have to Tell You?

Dr. Seuss's first book was rejected twenty-seven times.

Henry Ford's ideas were rejected by his father, his boss, his associates, and his partners until he went out on his own at the age of forty.

J.K. Rowling saw herself as *"the biggest failure I knew."* Her marriage had failed, she was jobless with a dependent child, but she described her failure as liberating: *"Rock bottom became a solid foundation on which I rebuilt my life."*

Paulo Coelho, author of *The Alchemist*, one of the best-selling books of all time, was committed to a mental institution three times.

Laura Ingalls Wilder, author of the *Little House on the Prairie* series, didn't write her first book until age sixty-five.

And of course, Grandma Moses's first canvas was painted at the age of seventy-six.

September 2

It Matters More than You Think

In every battle, there comes a time when both sides consider themselves beaten, then he who continues the attack wins.

—*Ulysses S. Grant*

He would know. After five generals had disappointed Lincoln, failing to bring the Civil War to an end, Grant forged ahead, refusing to accept defeat.

I asked a twenty-eight-year-old wealthy entrepreneur for his best success tip. He said, *Never give up. I had six businesses fail miserably before I finally had one success.*

I need to remember this on the days when I feel like it's no use or I have already tried everything.

It's not brains, talent, resources, or luck. It's tenacity.

And it sure helps to remember those who *persevered*—and made a big difference for many.

September 3

The Happiness Advantage ("CliffsNotes")

If you haven't watched Shawn Achor (a Harvard professor from Waco, Texas) talk about this yet on YouTube or Ted.com, here are the CliffsNotes:

In just two minutes a day, for twenty-one days straight, your brain can be rewired for continued happiness by just writing down three new gratitudes. Your brain will then retain a pattern of scanning the world for positive experiences instead of negatives.

Here are the five things recommended in Shawn's very popular Harvard class:

1. three gratitudes (think of three things for which you are grateful)
2. journaling (writing down one positive experience in the previous twenty-four hours will allow your brain the opportunity to relive it)
3. exercise (unfortunately, we all know this one)
4. meditation (allows your brain to rest)
5. random acts of kindness (as simple as sending out one praise or thank-you e-mail per day)

What will it hurt to try?

September 4

Reject Me—I Love it!

I read a book with this title by John Fuhrman two years ago and it helped me begin to use rejection to my advantage.

As a person who battled low self-esteem my entire life, the concept of "loving" rejection was radically foreign to me. Rejection sent me spiraling into the black hole—any type of rejection. Now, when I feel rejected I can look at it with healthy detachment.

- I acknowledge that I am still 100 percent valuable, regardless of someone else's opinion.
- I evaluate the rejection for lessons to be learned and then move on toward my goal.

I'm not perfect at it yet, but coming out of a funk sure takes less time than it used to.

Here's to a day of joy for us—*regardless!*

September 5

English Teachers Rock

When I was a sophomore in high school, I was very depressed, even suicidal. My English teacher, Mr. Springfield, noticed and talked with me after school. He suggested that I find one good thing to look forward to every day: a simple thing I could be happy about, like someone I was going to see or an outfit I was going to wear. He told me to let that one thing *carry me*.

I tried it. In my junior year in high school, my nickname became *Smiley*.

This simple exercise became one of the foundations for my positive nature today. The minute my eyes open, I begin to think of *everything* for which I am grateful, rather than the things I am worried about.

It wasn't brain surgery—*but* it changed my brain.

September 6

Hail to Underappreciated Authority Figures

During my last two years of high school, I was allowed to do a daily devotional message on the intercom, along with my friend Jackie, who did the announcements—until we had an on-the-air, full-blown argument about *the necessity of baptism for salvation.* Oops.

At that point, our principal came tearing down the hall with a look of horror on his face. After he ripped the microphone away from us, we were banned from the school intercom forever.

At the time, we thought he was such an insensitive, atheistic jerk! (How little credit rational authority figures receive.)

Now I know how desperately I need "principals" in the form of critics, rejection letters, bosses, and various recalcitrant relatives to add balance and maturity to my life.

What insight they can bring.

September 7

I Just "Kant"!

A steady guide for honest actions and the navigation through difficult moral questions is Immanuel Kant's *Categorical Imperative* statement: "Act as if the maxim of your action were to become, through your will, a Universal Law of Nature."

In other words, as Jostein Gaarder points out in *Sophie's World,* "when I do something, I must make sure that I want everyone else to do the same if they are in the same situation."

It's a different way of stating the Golden Rule, but it packs a particular punch in tight fixes.

This came to mind because I was giving thanks for the freedom of a clear conscience—having *absolutely nothing to hide from any other being or entity on earth.*

Kant's work is all about that freedom.

September 9

You Go, *Big Ben*!

Life is too short to be little.

—*Benjamin Disraeli*

- Walk, talk, and think like a champion (especially after a failure or disappointment)
- Concentrate on your assets (not your liabilities or weaknesses)
- Think about what's working (instead of what's not working)
- Forgive everyone
- Forget small inconveniences
- Smile
- Take risks

If you need some inspiration, read about how Benjamin Disraeli boldly turned his life into history.

When we decide not to be *little*, the world benefits!

September 10

Learners and Knowers

My husband, Bernie, always encourages his employees to be learners instead of *knowers*.

I now see that I spent too much of my life as a *knower* instead of a learner.

Learners are less opinionated. Learners hear others' opinions about themselves without getting defensive. Learners seek correction. Learners know that friends see our issues but don't tell us the truth for fear of hurting our feelings. Learners learn from their critics because critics aren't afraid of hurting our feelings.

Gee! How much faster could I have understood myself if I had learned from my "enemies" instead of defending myself against their words?

In seeking wisdom thou art wise; in imagining that thou hast attained it—thou art a fool.

—*Lord Chesterfield*

September 11

Every Day is 9/11 for Somebody

Such a sad day for the United States.

But all around the world, there are so many similar sad days to remember: days of genocide, terrifying natural disasters, terrorist attacks, war, brutality, disease and death. Our own 9/11 did change us by making us more aware of our vulnerability. My hope is that it also will make us more sensitive to the suffering of our brothers and sisters outside our borders.

"And who is my brother?"

To this question, Jesus answered with the story of the Good Samaritan. The man in the story was good because he was compassionate *outside his borders,* while others worried about proper boundaries, failing to offer the desperately needed assistance and love to a stranger.

May 9/11 teach us many things.

Blessed are they that mourn for they shall be comforted.

—*Jesus*

The Odds Are with the Bold

Avoiding danger is no safer in the long run than outright exposure. The fearful are caught as often as the bold.

—*Helen Keller*

Excessive concern for security freezes us.

—*Henri Nouwen*

In other words, *what have I got to lose?* Or, if I go to great ends to save myself, will I have anything worth saving?

I admit that I am a natural coward, and being bold is not easy for me.

But I can think of countless personal instances where *boldness* came through with great rewards, and *not one* where being a coward actually did.

Do the math. The odds are with the bold.

September 13

I'm New Here!

I don't know what to do! I'll pay for this! I'm new here!

Joe Dirt (tragically unsuccessful wildcatter)

Most of us have heard a similar voice in our head that says, "You don't know what the heck you're doing. They're going to find out you are a fraud any day now!"

My husband had a telling dream. While visiting a store that had the appearance of a carnival, he introduced himself to an eight-foot clown on stilts: "Hi, I'm the VP of Operations."

The clown responded, while shaking his hand, "So am I!" (Oh, what wisdom lurks in our subconscious!)

The point for me is this: If we own our inadequacies and insecurities but commit to a courageous path *in spite of them*, we win.

September 14

No Easy Answers

(A poem, written when my son, Hudson, was nine)

My son stands outside the back door
In my dream
Before I let him in, I say
What's that in your hands
There, behind your back?
Nothing, Mom.
But from his eyes, he says,
The blood and water of our ancestors, of course,
Pulsing with the thrill of discovery,
The heat of the kill and
The chill of deception
And oh, so many other things.
You know that, Mom.
I have all of this and so much more,
In this elaborate and delicate cage of time.
With complicated love, I inch the door open and let him in
Straining for a moment to see all he conceals.
He flies down the hall and
I hear him
Disappear into his future.

September 15

Your Sweet (and Not So Sweet) Side

You don't always show your sweet side.

—Lucinda Williams (singer, songwriter)

None of us do.

The song, honestly and passionately sung by Lucinda Williams, is an insightful expository of the *scars* that often precede the actions.

What I like about this song is the reminder that we are all a mixed bag. It has been useful in my relationships with others to be aware of this fact.

Relationship benefits:

- less pointing the finger
- less gossip
- less anger
- less hiding
- more honesty
- better boundaries
- more sleep

September 16

Daily Stretch

A person's mind, stretched to a new idea, never goes back to its original dimension.

—Oliver Wendell Holmes

It's so easy to do this with a book or an audio, a TED video a day, or, oh so many other options.

If I commit to a daily stretch, these are the possible benefits:

- I won't be a bigot.
- I will be more interesting to others.
- I won't be bored.
- I won't be small-minded.
- I will *grow* until I die and won't be an old, cranky person.

And the cool thing is that, as with physical exercise, I'll feel better about myself.

Forgiveness Technique

Catherine Ponder, author of *The Dynamic Laws of Prosperity*, suggests using a forgiveness technique for those of us who may be missing good things in our lives due to the harboring of ill feelings.

The technique is simple: Sit for half an hour every day and mentally forgive everyone that you are out of harmony with, have bad feelings toward, or are concerned about. If you have accused anyone of injustice, if you have discussed anyone unkindly, if you have criticized or gossiped about anyone, if you are legally involved with anyone, mentally ask their forgiveness.

Thirty minutes every day may seem like a long time, but our personal prosperity is probably worth the investment. Ponder says it is step one for bringing all the good we desire into our lives.

September 18

What Lessons Crazy Dreams Bring!

In the nineteenth century, George Mueller started a much-needed English orphanage *with only fifty cents in his pocket.* The orphanage grew to accommodate thousands of orphans.

During the Depression, Dorothy Day started a soup kitchen *with her rent money* and went on to establish many more all over the world.

Last night, I had this bizarre and intense dream that my life and the lives of two girls in my care were in extreme danger. Then, just at the right time, two armed FBI agents showed up to help. Yeah, right.

But—I woke with the assurance that *everything* I need will *always* be available when I need it.

Dorothy Day and George Mueller came to mind because they bravely lived their extraordinary and impactful lives with that confidence.

And what a difference it made.

September 19

Driving With a Full Tank

It's very subconscious, but I just realized that *I enjoy driving more when my tank is full of gas. I was not even aware but my brain was dealing with the pressure* of not running out of gas, the price of gas, having to stop, and maybe, if I had enough money to pay for the gas, etc.

That's lots of subconscious garbage!

This may be one of the most convincing arguments I have ever thought of for repeating daily affirmations—because—*the principle is the same.*

When my "spiritual tank" is full of gas, my mind rests. I have just relieved the pressure.

Affirmations program my brain by telling it

1. I have everything I need;
2. all is well; and
3. *the tank is full!*

Now I can enjoy the ride!

September 20

Don't Bore Yourself

I not only use all the brains that I have, but all that I can borrow.

—Woodrow Wilson

I don't know about you, but if I am not reading or listening to smart people, I become a pretty boring person. According to the honest people in my life, I also become a whiner, a nagger, tedious, and insensitive.

I didn't read my first book until I was in the seventh grade. I went to my first public library in the eleventh grade. I didn't start reading the great classics until my mid-twenties. I was too selective about what I read until my late forties.

I'm making up for lost time now, but can always tell when I'm not borrowing enough brains:

I bore myself!

September 21

All is Well

A big turning point in my life came when I quit *trying* to be successful and realized *I was already successful.*

I had spent all my savings, other people's savings, and money *I didn't have* to make a film that flopped. I then wrote more stuff and kept sending it out, hoping for someone to affirm my talent, and help me recoup my investment.

Nothing happened—*other than this:*

One day, peace washed over me as I realized what fun I was having being an entrepreneur, utilizing my gifts. I remember thinking, "It doesn't matter if my work gets produced. I am doing what I was born to do. Someone will benefit from my work and it is okay if I die broke."

Life has never been better!

September 22

A Little Honesty Goes a Long Way

At a convention in Las Vegas, I mentioned to my audience that I had struggled with lying since the age of five. Raised by a screamer, I had considered it a necessary survival skill. More than one person approached me afterward with a tearful confession of the same propensity.

For some of us, needed breakthroughs come only when someone else admits to sharing our own carefully hidden pain.

I was eighteen before I began telling the truth. It's gotten easier as I become more comfortable with being human. Now I know that the *only thing* that could keep me from enjoying love and acceptance is my own dishonesty.

September 23

Not Derailed

I delivered a workshop, and many people come up afterward to tell me what a difference it had made for them.

Then, while in the restroom, I overheard two ladies saying negative things about me.

In the past, I would have focused on their comments and decided that the day had been a failure. I would have beat myself up all the way home, trying to figure out how I could have done a better job. Then, I would be depressed.

But not now.

Today, I say, "I am making a difference. I will improve as I go. I will focus on the good, the encouraging and the hopeful."

Optimism is the faith that leads to achievement. Nothing can be done without hope and confidence.

—*Helen Keller*

100 Percent Valuable

Melissa, a seminar participant, told me that she had overheard a coffee shop server being yelled at by a customer, so she went over to the server and said, "Don't let this incident get you down. You are 100 percent valuable right now." The server brightened up and was very grateful for the kind and timely words.

Melissa had just heard those words during the morning session of my seminar. She made a point to tell me that the class had immediate value and usefulness for her.

Melissa was a conduit of good and reminded me that I had been a conduit as well. I will tell my friend Debbie that she had been a conduit when, last week, *she told me* that I was 100 percent valuable.

September 25

I'm Thankful—*But*

Giving thanks should always raise our spirits—but it doesn't always do so. It doesn't because, we are thinking, "I'm thankful, but, I really need such and such to happen," or, "I'm thankful, but my life sucks."

This will *never* do for gratitude! Gratitude that brings happiness and change in your life doesn't have the *"but."*

The *"but"* can only be removed by reprogramming your body and mind to *feel grateful.* Many times, I have sat in my car, turned up the radio loud, and sung with all of my strength until I felt happier. I have made myself dance until I felt like dancing! And I have jumped up and down until I felt healthy and joyful!

Then, gratitude comes.

(Fake it until you make it.)

September 26

Closer to My Ideal Self

I deal with everyone as if their heart is breaking.

—*Rebecca Dunn (former North Dakota Congresswoman)*

When Rebecca Dunn was asked to explain the secret behind her power, this quote was her answer. This baffled me at first, until I realized that everyone's heart is breaking, or has broken, or will break. Being sensitive to that helps me deal as *sensitive equals* with *everyone*.

- If someone appears arrogant and pushy, I think of their broken heart and I am not intimidated by them.
- If someone appears weak or timid, I think of their broken heart, and I am more careful with them.
- If someone is oblivious, I think of their broken heart, and am more patient.

And reverence for another's experience always brings me closer to my ideal self.

September 27

When I Screwed Up

Sometimes, I can't sleep or wake up thinking about *that thing* I wish I hadn't said or done. At that point, I have to make a quick move or I'll go into a sucking spiral of self-hatred and/or replaying the event over in my mind, *ad infinitum.*

The *quick move* is to ask myself, "Is there anything I can do to fix it?" and if there isn't, to be sincerely grateful for the learning experience, acknowledge my humanity, and think about things I did right. Otherwise, my day will be colored in deathly gray tones instead of the beautiful, intense hues of a life *lived completely in the moment.*

September 28

Well-Worn Dependency

History shows that every type of institution and organization fails, and the individual is exposed. Have a plan for your life so that you are not dependent on any institution.

—Tom Butler-Bowden *(author of 50 Best Self-Help Classics)*

Many years ago, a friend suggested to me that working for myself might be an option. I thought she was out of her mind. I had to have that paycheck! When I later started my own business, *it was because no one would hire me and I had no choice.* But I am glad I took the plunge. I didn't know that I could have been using my gifts before—without the endorsement of any institution.

For personal development *or* financial security, getting out of well-worn dependency is usually the wisest and *safest* path.

September 29

The Beginning Is Near!

I am not fond of sports analogies because sometimes they seem so trite when compared with the real battle of life. *But*—while playing golf the other day, I shot four really bad holes in a row. It was only going from bad to worse until I realized I could start over on the next hole and forget about the annoying score. I parred the next four holes.

I came home and started over on a failed (and formerly discouraging) project.

The most successful person is the one who is best at processing failure.

—James Allen *(As a Man Thinketh)*

September 30

Call for Noble Hearts and Minds

The brave men, living and dead, who struggled here, have consecrated it far above our poor power to add or detract.

—*Abraham Lincoln (within the Gettysburg address)*

The absolute power of this address is that it expressed Lincoln's complete awareness of the value of human life.

I keep a copy of it on my desk as a quick entry into that *noble frame of mind.*

I read it in only two and a half minutes and it *never fails* to move me to

- noble thought and action;
- a desire to live on a higher plane;
- reverence for those who have dedicated their lives to higher aims; and
- gratitude for those few who see past themselves and their own agendas.

I want to be that kind of person.

October

Balance

A person maintains his balance, poise, and sense of security only as he is moving forward.

—Dr. Maxwell Maltz

A well-developed sense of humor is the pole that adds balance to your steps as you walk the tightrope of life.

—William Arthur Ward

October 1

A Balancing Act

And she balanced in the delight of her thought,
A wren, happy, tail to the wind

—Theodore Roethke

My friend Mary sent this poem in a card, and it reminded me of the power our thoughts have to transport us—wherever we want to go.

When circumstances challenge me, I must *balance in the delight of my thought.*

People who practice Neuro-Linguistic Programing (NLP) recommend the association of a hearty laugh or a joke, for instance, to a bad memory, so that every time the memory comes, so does the hearty laugh or the joke. This is one way we can balance *in the delight of a thought* and reclaim the power over our lives and direction.

So, if you hear me laughing, it may be part of my balancing act.

October 2

Normal Is Overrated

My favorite line from the movie *Soul Surfer*, about Bethany Hamilton becoming a professional surfer *after* a shark bit off her arm is her mother's consolation to her: "Normal is overrated."

It is.

Growing up, I always felt *abnormal*. I wish I had rejoiced in that instead of fretted about it, because all the *abnormalities* in my life have now become my unique voice.

I saw a story this week about a middle-aged housewife who became an escape artist. (I wonder how she discovered the talent. Hmmmm.)

Isn't that abnormal? But she sure looked happy about her new life! She said she hoped her life would inspire others to find their hidden talents.

I hope you will own *your* normal—*not someone else's*.

October 3

Too Simple for You?

Positive thinking will let you do everything better than negative thinking will.

—*Zig Ziglar*

Until a few years ago, I thought Zig Ziglar was a simpleton, until I started using his suggested daily affirmations.

His message may be simple, but his recommendations work!

I am often amazed how we refuse to do something as simple as say positive things to ourselves and about ourselves every day. We would rather continue to moan and groan about our lives.

And, as we dig deeper into the negativity, those who refuse to do so continue to rise above their circumstances.

Step one—Take a twenty-four-hour challenge today: *No negative thoughts or words.*

Step two—Substitute *positive statements* such as, "I am happy to be alive today," or "I am healthy, successful, joyful, and loving."

October 4

Run for Your Life! The *Words* Are Coming!

Sticks and stones can break my bones but words can never harm me.

This childhood taunt is simply not true!

Words are blunt, brutal instruments that bludgeon our confidence and morale and, even more frightening, leave behind little *worms* that crawl into our brain, reprogram it, and then eat away our futures.

And not just the words of insensitive enemies—our own words will do the same damage, *unless* we are careful to only think and speak positively.

Because my brain's *only* job is to help me avoid pain and experience pleasure, it is constantly and carefully listening to what I tell it about the world. When I speak only good, my world *improves*.

We may not be able to control what others say—but we can *always* control the commentary!

October 5

The Ubiquitous Power of the *First Time*

All my life, I've looked at words as though I were seeing them for the first time.

—*Ernest Hemingway*

Hmmmm. Maybe that was why he had such a *way* with words and a sincere appreciation for their power, purpose, and uniqueness.

Last night, I looked at the moon as if for the first time—talk about cutting-edge artistic lighting! It changes colors, shapes, and even its location!

This morning I looked at my desk, my dog, and my bathroom sink *as if for the first time.*

Now, looking at the people in my life, *as if for the first time* (as Hemingway with words), I am able to work with them with greater ease and pleasure.

Oh, the ubiquitous power of *first-time delight!*

October 6

Painful Eagerness of Unfed Hope

Not so long ago, I felt a continuous, nagging pain in my core. The pain was that of loneliness, despair, confusion, and rejection. I felt that my potential was trapped inside me without hope of any outlet. I felt destined to the pain of an isolated and mediocre existence. It was a deep mental pain, but so real, it was visceral. I'm sure many of you can relate.

I only think of it now to

- *rejoice* that is a very remote memory;
- *remind* myself that so many others are in this place; and
- *recognize* my ability to alleviate that suffering, today, for others.

Speak hope to people in your path today.

What we call our despair is often only the painful eagerness of unfed hope.

—*George Eliot*

October 7

It's a Game, Not a Battle

If we want war, we'll get war. If we want fun, we'll get fun.

We tell our brains how to perceive our days and our challenges.

If you're not sure about the validity of this assertion, keep this in mind: *we are so much more fun to be around if we are playing, rather than fighting.*

I'm talking about being *drama-free:* letting go of criticism, complaints, and negativity and choosing to be nonreactive to the ego in others. What do we have to lose?

Headaches, shoulder pain, back ache, tics, uneasiness, fear, sleeplessness, and tension. Nothing else.

Drama never got us anywhere, anyway.

Just try it today—for your health, or at least, for the sake of your friends!

I fed my ego, but not my soul.

—*Yakov Smirnoff*

October 8

Expect Change

I left before dawn this morning to run a 5K in Oklahoma, and I forgot to write my blog the night before.

No excuse, just an oversight. But, while typing these words, I remembered that, just a few years ago, these words would not have been in my vocabulary.

Blog? 5K? Me?

Also, tennis, 10K, half-marathon, world travel, webinars, keynotes, writing books and screenplays, and many, many other *"foreign"* terms.

In Dr. David Burns's book, *Feeling Good,* about cognitive therapy, he makes the point that humans are *never* stagnant entities, but ever-evolving, defying definitive labels. This is important to remember when we feel depressed or unhappy with ourselves and make pronouncements such as, "I'm a loser" or "I'm a total failure."

All is subject to change.

Wait for it.

The Convincing Little Things

Some moments leave a lifelong impression on us.

I had taken a wrong turn on the way to the airport and gotten stuck in downtown Washington DC's rush-hour gridlock. Missing my plane would mean a costly inconvenience for several people. I felt my fear rising, so I called my friend Mary Brouillette and asked her to pray for me.

I have no earthly idea how this happened, but when I looked up, there was a clear and easy path ahead of me. Where had the cars gone? I still cannot explain how I was at the airport within a few minutes.

But times like this convince me that *faith always trumps fear.*

Don't believe in miracles; depend on them.

—*Laurence J. Peter*

October 10

To Be Wildly Useful

I watched *Basketball Diaries* last night. Like *Requiem for a Dream*, the story cuts into the mind, helping the watcher grasp the distinction of pleasure from *joy*.

A good reminder for me.

When I pursue pleasure, I go to bed feeling a little empty. But when I pursue the joy that comes from using my gifts and being productive, I lay my head down at night with contentment—and experience great pleasure *as a side benefit*.

This doesn't mean that I don't play. I play more—but with the purpose of being healthy, balanced, rested, and renewed so that I can be *wildly useful* to myself and others!

When the mind is pure, joy follows like a shadow that never leaves.

—*Buddha*

October 11

Internal Dialogue Check

This morning, as I began to write, my first thoughts were negative about my abilities. It's not surprising that a feeling of dread (about a day of writing query letters) came over me.

But.

I annihilated that feeling of dread instantaneously by saying out loud, "This is my calling and it has helped others. What fun I'll have today doing what I was born to do."

Honestly, I felt genuinely happy and motivated by my next breath!

Whatever happens today, I can now enjoy it—all because of a simple adjustment to *my internal dialogue*.

If you have no confidence in yourself, you are twice defeated in the race of life. With confidence, you have won even before you have started.

— *Marcus Tullius Cicero*

That's what I'm talking about!

October 12

Failures Are *Only* Installment Payments

Failure is nothing but success trying to be born in a bigger way. Most seeming failures are just installments toward victory!

—*Catherine Ponder*

Countless times in my past, I have been guilty of saying, "I tried, but it didn't work," and I have used that as an excuse for quitting.

What I now understand is that people who "make it" in their field of dreams do so because they *refuse* to take no as a permanent answer!

Today, I take the advice of countless sages and laugh at rejection by saying, "I'm just one more 'no' closer to yes! Nothing can stop me from living the life I was born to live and giving the gifts I was born to give! Yea!"

October 13

Do People in Your Life a Favor

When I was eighteen, I made a commitment to center myself every morning before my day began. I've been benefiting from this practice for decades now.

Of course, there have been days that I didn't think I had time to calm and feed my spirit and, unfortunately, people in my life usually paid the price. But I could justify it this way:

"Is it my fault if I don't make it to my center? No! It is the fault of those pesky centrifugal forces throwing me hard against the outer wall of my existence."

Today, I don't buy that excuse, and I am aware that being centered is the most important gift I will give to others today.

October 14

When Circumstances Are Less Than Ideal

You cannot travel within and stand still without.

—*James Allen*

If you want change in your outward circumstances, invest in your inner world.

There is always a payoff for this, *even if you can't see it at the time.*

As a consultant, I've seen many disgruntled employees remove obstacles and quickly change their standing at work by doing these simple things:

- Refusing to complain about conditions.
- Complimenting and praising more.
- Arriving with a smile—and keeping it.
- Saying *"Yes"* more often.
- Being positive about change.
- Remembering that negativity always hurts somebody.

Today, whether it is work or politicians, our kids or our parents, our partners or our friends—we can have a positive effect on all these outer worlds by changing *our* inner world.

Your joy is in your hands!

October 15

Are You a Raving, Abusive, Immature, Narcissistic Parent to Yourself?

When balanced, mature, conscientious, and loving parents think of their kids,

1. they think of how much they love them;
2. they delight in their potential; and
3. they rack their brains thinking about what they can do to help them.

And then, way down on the *bottom* of the list, they think about how their kids might be screwing up.

I get much better results from myself when I treat myself with the care of a balanced, mature, conscientious, and loving parent.

Unfortunately, I spent many years treating myself as a raving, immature, narcissistic, and abusive parent would, starting with the last item and *never getting to the first three.*

October 16

Simple Prescription

God measures souls by their capacity for entertaining his best angel, love.

—*Ella Wheeler Wilcox*

In fact, *consciously or unconsciously*, love interests, friends, bosses, coworkers, family, and even strangers measure us this way too.

If you are not sure this is the case, do an experiment:

Wherever life is "failing you" today, wherever you are pained, troubled, complacent, or unhappy, replace fear, anger, resentment, boredom, or uneasiness with love. Start doing that by thinking and making only loving statements about yourself, your situations, or the people in your life. Persist.

Then, watch the transformation occur.

Or, keep looking for more complicated solutions.

Or, keep doing what you have always done.

Angels are standing by.

October 17

Traffic Cop of Data

"What you just said screwed me up."

I overheard a girl say this to her father who was coaching her golf swing, and, after I chuckled, I thought about how vulnerable humans are to what others put into our heads.

In fact, as in our dream lives, our waking lives will become merely an expression of those words we have passively collected and stored *unless* we take counter measures. If we want the *composite* that is our life to be more than the sum of the random parts, we must become *the traffic cop of the data.*

Clear, sort, and replace every day.

Quiet, reflective meditative reading and thought will balance your day—and your life.

Small investment, big payoff—the complete, total, and remarkable (*less* screwed-up) *you.*

October 18

You Said It; I Needed It

Sometimes you find unexpected resonance with a writer. I wrote the following poem about that.

Surprised by pathos
undiscovered until now
my body writhes with recognition
my eyes fill with the tears of kinship
as I read and drink the power of the ages
the words of the wind
the current of the heart
drank from this earthen jar
passed from lip to lip
to my prepared heart
aching with life
on this familiar road.

My soul fills every inch of my physical space
pressing against the walls
enlarging my capacity
increasing my surface area of connection to the world.
I feel the heat of the sun in my hair
I am conscious of my stretching body
stretching toward truth
stretching toward discovery
and finally
peace.

October 19

Music to the Rescue

Music satisfies and nourishes the hunger within ourselves for connection and harmony.

—*Cat Stevens*

We all know that music has power.

But did you know it can be used to heal relationships?

As a good movie soundtrack "nourishes" the action and pulls our emotions into the story, so music can work subtly to harmonize relationships.

Here is an example:

When I am having trouble with someone, I put a "soundtrack" behind my thoughts about them. I play a favorite song, and, while it plays, I think of the person in a non-judgmental way. I think about their innate value and imagine God working in their life.

This time spent "harmonizing" with them never fails to improve my attitude.

And when *my* attitude improves, change occurs.

October 20

Semi-Broken Receptacles

It is not difficult to honor, value, and respect *every* human being *equally* (regardless of status, looks, wealth, origin, etc.) if we are aware that every last one of us is a transient, semi-broken receptacle of seemingly random experience, making decisions based on ridiculously limited information, trying to make it through life with the least amount of pain. Some of us fare better than others. All of us are in different stages of the journey. *All are subject to change.*

When I walk through a crowd of people, I feel the significance of each individual in that crowd, whether it is the janitor or the governor, and I am honored by their presence.

October 21

The Forgiving State of Mind

The forgiving state of mind is a magnetic power for attracting good.

—*Catherine Ponder*

In *The Dynamic Laws of Prosperity,* Ponder instructs us to send positive thoughts toward those who have wronged us: to bless them and watch the blessings begin to flow into our lives. She reminds us that *denouncement usually backfires.* True forgiveness *never* does.

This is not new stuff! Jesus said it, Buddha said it. Your grandmother probably said it, too.

But we think we know better and that person doesn't deserve forgiveness. That person deserves punishment, and we're going to pray that God gives it to them!

I'm just saying that, if you want to attract good into your life today, you must give out good to *all.*

Don't Be a Hazard to Yourself!

I love the Pink song, *Don't Let Me Get Me*, because the words reflect precisely the way I used to feel about myself.

As Pink expresses in her lyrics, I also felt I was my own worst enemy, I wanted to be somebody else, and I fought a war against the mirror.

But today, thanks to helpful friends, I no longer feel this way!

One of those friends is Mary Brouillette, whose remedy for self-criticism is counterattack. When she sees a flaw in herself, she says, "Yeah, but, _____ (naming something positive about herself instead)."

Try it.

It certainly helps everyone if we befriend ourselves.

October 23

"Bad" Judgment

A mistake in judgment isn't fatal, but too much anxiety about judgment is.

—*Pauline Kael*

Okay, I've been wrong many times in my *I-know-I'm-right* judgment of people, places, and facts. But beating myself up for it won't get me anywhere today. I just have to admit my mistake, chalk it up as a learning experience (no matter how many times I've made the same mistake), and move on.

And it is sweet release to let it go.

I know some mistakes in judgment costs lives. Some cost only humiliation, money, or inconvenience. Either way, *not forgiving* ourselves will cause

1. hiding;
2. self-righteousness;
3. self-hatred;
4. lying;
5. extension of our pain onto others; and
6. a plethora of neurotic and psychotic disorders.

October 24

"Bad" Judgment, Part Two

Irony is a clear consciousness of an eternal agility, of the infinitely abundant chaos.

—*Karl Wilhelm Friedrich Schlegel*

The abundant irony in life instructs us in many ways. One of the elementary lessons is that our judgment is not as airtight as we think.

So, the other day, I was looking forward to doing one thing and dreading another. The task I was dreading turned out to be the highlight of my day, and the event I was excited about was, surprisingly, the low point.

Today I'm going to count on irony.

I'm going to relax, quit taking myself so seriously, and look forward to *everything*. I'll remember that pain is sometimes joy and joy is sometimes pain, and that gain is sometimes loss and loss is sometimes gain.

Surprise!

October 25

Simply Because It Is an Honor

Do you remember the movie *Groundhog Day*? Bill Murray's character is doomed to repeat one day over and over until he gets it right. When he finally gets it right, he is *genuine* and *caring* toward his romantic interest, and she finds him absolutely irresistible.

Unfortunately, many of us continue to repeat bad relationships as if we were stuck in a *Groundhog Day*-type-of-experience. We blame the other party for our problems, because we have refused to love simply and purely, with no strings attached.

Drop the agenda, and relate to people as if it is an honor to be in their presence—*because it is!* Quit thinking about what you should get back from them.

And watch the transformation take place.

(From *The Miracle I Almost Missed*)

October 26

Reject Dis-ease! Quit Complaining

When I complain about someone or something, it is *never* constructive. *All* negativity toward my present reality will dilute my intent for change in the future. This doesn't mean that I have to pretend. It just means that I accept the present moment *as it is*. Then, I can set my intention toward a better future—with a willingness to take action if necessary.

With this approach, I retain my joy and peace and reject *dis-ease:* the *dis-ease* which leads to heart attacks, anxiety, depression, illness, and lots of other painful stuff.

So, today, I consciously choose not to trash–talk *anyone or anything* (including politicians, the weather, or celebrities).

Intention combined with detachment leads to life-centered, present-moment awareness ... Accept the present and intend the future. Never struggle against the present.

—*Deepak Chopra*

October 27

In Search of a Miracle?

Three daily steps for finding miracles:

1. *Refuse* to lose hope, particularly if you feel that life has passed you by.
2. *Remember* that you are the *miracle* that someone else is looking for.
3. *Repeat* this affirmation when you get discouraged:

"Someone out there is waiting for me to be the *miracle* in his or her life! My challenges today are preparation for that encounter."

The bigger the challenge, the greater the *miracle!*

(From *The Miracle I Almost Missed*)

Hold on, I'm coming.

—*Sam and Dave*

October 28

Can You Hear the Music?

Years ago, I met a delightful retired couple, Nanny and Papa, who became very dear to our family. When Papa died of a painful lung disease, Nanny, after fifty-five years of marriage, was unusually peaceful. She told us why.

"Papa was in terrible pain and was in and out of consciousness. But, right before he died, his face lit up and he became very lucid. He said, 'Nanny, can you hear the music? Isn't it beautiful?' He then died with an angelic smile on his face."

You may be skeptical about this story and many others like it, but you cannot deny the extraordinary, transcendent power of music to give hope.

When you need a boost today, I hope that you will *hear the music.*

It's playing in your soul.

October 29

Let Yourself Out of Prison

Stop everything you are doing right now. Stop plotting, worrying, and running around. Something is missing in your external *and internal* flurry of activity—*you:* the essential, unique, complete, and joyful *you*.

It takes less time than a shower and fulfills the same purpose *internally:* a simple *daily* routine of quiet (meditation, prayer, reading, music—whatever gets you there).

But, if we sincerely want to turn on our best lives, we must do it, today. We must abruptly stop and tap into our true spiritual self, the self that is untainted by the taskmasters of the ego and self-imposed expectations.

The distinctive features of everyday mediocre existence are helplessness, hopelessness, mundane needs, trivial concerns, quiet desperation, and seriousness. Healthy detachment from our own agenda frees us from this prison.

—*Deepak Chopra* (Chopra 2000)

October 30

Send Dreams, Not Nightmares

All that we send into the lives of others comes back into our own.

—*Edward Markham*

All.

Keeping this in mind will propel you to service and honesty, influence how you treat others, and possibly change the way you talk about people, too.

In the last few years of my mother's life, she began to tell me about a "bitchy, mean woman" who was stalking her. At first, I thought this woman was real. Then, I realized that my mother was fighting off the demons of her own bitterness and experiencing a *personification* of this quote.

Nothing you send out is lost. Good deeds (as well as bad words) will *stalk* the originator of them.

And you never know when and how they will show up.

Send dreams, not nightmares.

October 31

Costume or Not, I See You

I always felt invisible as a child, as if I had no real importance or significance to other people. So, besides the candy, this was the reason I really liked Halloween. Even adults would react to me and talk to me when I had a costume on!

This feeling of being invisible as a child left a lifelong impression upon me. I am acutely sensitive to the pain someone has when they feel unseen.

Nobody is nobody.

—Bernie Beck

Manners are a sensitive awareness of the feelings of others. If you have that awareness, you have good manners, no matter what fork you use.

—Emily Post

November

Insight

A moment's insight is sometimes worth a life's experience.

—Oliver Wendell Holmes Jr.

November 1

November, Nowvember

Happy brand new month to you! So what's it going to be? Choose your theme.

November will be my _____ (kindness, fitness, reading, learning, sharing, growing, laughing, etc.) month.

Movember in New Zealand and Australia is a very big *mustache-growing-fund-raiser for men's health.* The movement has spread to Canada and is creeping into the US. What I like about this campaign is the theme and direction it gives to November. *It makes November more than just a getting-ready-for-the-holidays month.*

Why not make this a pivotal month of change and awareness for our own lives? Why wait until January to set a new direction? *Newvember, Nowvember it is!*

There is only one moment in time when it is essential to awaken. That moment is Now(vember).

—*Buddha (modified)*

November 2

Nowvember Report

My *Now*vember theme is to listen more and blurt less. By the end of the month, I want to have made significant progress keeping my lips buttoned up.

This morning, while visiting with a new friend, I talked and talked, and it wasn't until the end of the chat that I realized that she had a very interesting story to tell. *I wished I had given her some airspace much earlier in the conversation.*

Yesterday, I blurted out my opinion too quickly, and I hurt someone's feelings by not "hearing" that person first.

Wisdom is the reward you get for a lifetime of listening when you'd have preferred to talk.

—*Doug Larson*

November 3

Buck Brannaman Sings His Song

You could write a song about some kind of emotional problem you are having, but it would not be a good song, in my eyes, until it went through a period of sensitivity to a moment of clarity. Without that moment of clarity to contribute to the song, it's just complaining.

—*Joni Mitchell*

The world has enough complaining.

Buck is a documentary about the real horse whisperer. His story is one of abuse and heartache, but he found clarity through it and used that clarity to bring kindness and healing to horses and their owners. Buck Brannaman is just an average man who makes a remarkable difference using his hard-earned clarity.

Clarity or complaints?

What song will you sing today?

November 4

Holy Irony!

Because dwelling from, not upon, the space you want to inherit is the fastest way to change absolutely everything.

—Mike Dooley (Notes from the Universe)

I'm *finally* beginning to understand this about faith—and prayer—and positive thinking—and the Law of Attraction: to manifest my longings, I must not be longing. (*Ultimate irony.*) I must be there already!

Faith is to be light with joy and peace. No heaviness of spirit. No sighing. No I'm happy, *but* I wish this or that would hurry up and happen. No anything else at all. Only that feeling of fruition, completion, contentment, and fulfillment.

This spirit is so attractive. It not only draws people to us, it draws a universe of good to us as well, because the entire universe has been created and programmed with and by this *holy spirit*.

November 5

Focus Adjustment

We become *exactly* what we focus on. It's a law of the universe.

Focus on disappointments, become a disappointment.

Focus on possibilities, become a miracle.

Focus on unhappy things, become unhappy.

Focus on role models, become a role model.

Focus on petty things, become petty.

Focus on noble things, become a noble and courageous human being who lives a *worthy* life.

What are you becoming today? It's never too late to become the hero of your dreams.

November 6

Newvember, Nowvember Time

Know how to live the time that is given you.

—*Dario Fo*

I used to get so nervous on Sundays, knowing I had to go back to work or school the next day. This ended up causing me wasted hours, spent in frustration, anger, and irritability with people and inefficiencies that threatened the commodity of my precious time.

Thoreau said, *"Time is but the stream I go a-fishing in."* This has helped me make friends with time, have a relaxed attitude toward it, and quit relating to it as a taskmaster.

With the advent of daylight saving time in the United States, we have one extra hour of daylight. This is just a reminder that we can *go fishin' in it* for all the things that give us joy, or we can just fret it away.

Now is the hour.

November 7

A Friend of *Mind*

It was a typo, but a good one.

We all need *a friend of mind:* a mind that will speak peace to us, remind us not to take ourselves too seriously and switch us from negative to positive.

Often our minds are not friendly to us. In fact, cognitive therapy has shown that much depression is caused by what we think—that negative thinking does not stem from depression but the other way around.

The good news is that optimism can be learned *at any stage* in our lives. Designating a day to practice is a first step.

Note of warning: when you are being optimistic, the pessimists or realists don't necessarily want you to try to be a friend of *their* minds.

November 8

Less Fear, Less Anger, More Strength

Whenever I am angry or upset it is usually about this: I am afraid that something valuable is being taken from me.

I experience much less anger in my life when I remember three things:

1. Every good thing is a gift, *not an entitlement.*
2. What I am afraid of losing, many never had in the first place.
3. No one can take my soul.

I'm not advocating becoming a doormat or ignoring my true feelings.

I am saying that anger doesn't usually accomplish my ends. If I am less angry, I have more power over my circumstances. And, most importantly, I cannot be less angry until I am more fearless—until I realize that I have *nothing* to lose.

All is well.

November 9

Cheap Face Lift

If you think something kind about anyone, say it. If you can't say it to them right now, write down a reminder to tell them later. This is one reason I like Facebook; it's easy to give compliments quickly.

Search through your thoughts. Are there any unsaid kindnesses lurking there? Let them out. I don't know anything that does as much good as telling someone that you noticed something good about them. It lifts at least two faces: theirs—*and yours*.

(And that could come in handy for the holidays.)

Everyone responds to kindness.

—*Richard Gere*

A little thought and a little kindness are often worth more than a great deal of money.

—*John Ruskin*

Same Song; Second Verse

You're so self-centered that you can't think about anyone else's feelings for a moment. Last time you came here—you talked and talked about yourself and never asked me one question.

Aliena's explanation for her rejection of William's proposal.

Pillars of the Earth by Ken Follett

Throughout world history, the story is always the same: for anyone, everyone, whoever, and in whatever situation to be well-liked, loved, happy, or successful, put others' needs before your own. Lose your life to find it. Give to receive.

This is the spirit, the law of the universe, the foundation of legends, and the secret of a satisfying life.

It doesn't mean that you despise or ignore yourself. It means you honor yourself as the noble creature you are.

November 11

One Day

Whatever you might think the 11/11 date means, I only know for sure that it means I didn't die in my sleep on 11/10, and I have *at least* one more chance to live my best life!

Whatever our superstitions are about this unusual date or whatever the circumstances today, we can choose to *really live* it; live it with all the spunk, power, audacity, laughter, love, and courage we can find. We are equal to *(or greater than)* whatever comes on 11.11.

Let's call it our lucky day and plan on having another one tomorrow.

Character is destiny.

—*Heraclitus*

Is There a Connection?

Don't expect to receive prosperity until you are giving freely of whatever you have—and you always have something to give.

—*Catherine Ponder*

We checked into a hotel and made an effort to really *see* the clerk. Without explanation, complimentary champagne was delivered to the hotel room.

In spite of our busy work schedule, we took time to notice all the service personnel, thank them, and tip generously.

The next day, on the way to the cheap seats at *Jersey Boys,* a woman ushered us, instead, to the front of the stage *with no explanation.*

Saturday night, instead of having a night out, we had dinner with a business owner who needed advice. On the way there, a complete stranger handed us free tenth-row tickets to Phantom of the Opera.

Luck or Law of Attraction?

November 13

Victim of Sinister Behavior or Casualty of Life's Experiments?

Everybody plays the fool sometimes. There's no exception to the rule.

—*Aaron Neville*

Someone recently described to me (in lurid detail) the sinister behavior of an ex, explaining how *everything* the person had done from the very beginning of their relationship had been calculated malevolence.

I do not doubt that this type of sinister behavior does exist—but it is *rare*. Most people do not spend their waking hours plotting your demise. They are too busy figuring out their own stuff to have time for that! We are all casualties of life's experiments.

And every one of us is a mixed bag of noble and ignoble, good intentions and broken promises, blessings and curses. Once we admit we are all in the same category, it is easier to forgive and move on.

November 14

Grow Up and Own Your Stuff

Gladly we desire to make other men perfect, but we will not amend our own fault.

—*Thomas Kempis*

I've said some pretty heartless, insensitive, judgmental, opinionated, and dogmatic things about my bosses, leaders, coworkers, family, friends, and strangers. Allowing myself to objectively remember those words and the harm they caused has become my primary motivation to forgive and disregard insults or hurts that have come from others.

I regret my rashness. I regret thinking that my vantage point was flawless. I regret thinking that I was the center of the universe.

I will not rationalize my oversights.

The least I can do to amend for them is to forgive the blunders of others.

Only then will I have *grown up.*

November 15

Hey, You Missed a Spot

My daughter said this to me as I was dusting a living room table. She was right. When I looked at the table from her angle, I could see it.

Sometimes, it seems that people are always telling us, "You missed a spot." It's not always easy to hear these words, especially from an armchair critic.

I finally figured out that there was no need to argue about it, though. Another person's opinion doesn't mean that he or she is a better person than I am, only that he or she sees things from a different angle.

No need to hold a grudge. No need to feel grieved about it.

Grief is the agony of an instant. The indulgence of grief the blunder of a life.

—*Benjamin Disraeli*

God, You Have Forgotten My Name

While in a period of deep disillusionment about my life, when I was driving to work one morning, I said out loud, "God, if you ever knew my name, you have forgotten it by now."

Coming toward me on the other side of the highway was an eighteen-wheeled truck with *PAM* written on the front cab and *PAM* in six-foot letters on the side of the trailer. I had *never*, in my entire life seen a *PAM* truck before. Since that day, I have seen hundreds of them. And on one day alone, thirty-eight *PAM* trucks passed me.

I got the message—and what a difference it has made.

November 17

Troublemaker or Trouble Shaker?

If you see oppression of the poor, and justice and righteousness trampled in a country, do not be astounded.

—*King Solomon*

It's a waste of our time to talk to others about how shocked we are. It is a waste of our time to gossip and complain about things being screwed up. What is not a waste of our time is to dedicate ourselves to becoming part of the solution. There are plenty of people to show disdain and keep up a running commentary. What is it that you can do? The first place to start is in your own airspace.

It is often easier to become outraged by injustice half a world away than by oppression and discrimination half a block from home.

—*Carl T. Rowan*

November 18

The Bright Light of *Wow*

Too often, we make excuses for not bringing ourselves totally to the moment. If you want to stay stuck then tell yourself, "I've been through a lot lately." "I can't just pretend I'm okay," or "People don't know what I'm going through and what I am dealing with right now."

Or, you can just show up and offer *all* that you are.

Be present for people, see them, get your focus off yourself and onto the amazing life around you. Sooner than you think, you'll change your world from the dull gray of barely-getting-by to the bright light of wow-I'm alive-for-a-reason.

November 19

Relatives

My mom said she learned how to swim when someone took her out in the lake and threw her off the boat. I said, "Mom, they weren't trying to teach you how to swim."

—*Paula Poundstone*

I thought you might need some family humor for the holidays.

And a few more tips:

- Don't take yourself so seriously.
- Don't worry about what anyone thinks about you.
- Savor.
- Be in the moment.
- See (people as if for the first time).
- Hear (only good about each other).
- Feel (alive).
- Smell (the morning, because you have one, and the food, because many don't).
- Taste (*every* bite).
- Have a great holiday!

November 20

Don't Tell Me He's Not Real!

The Geiko gecko—I'm in love with him. He's so humble and so vulnerable. He has the genuine desire to help—and that adorable Aussie accent.

I want to hear every word he has to say.

What a model of success for the advertising world.

Also, what a model for the character that makes us more adorable and lovable to strangers, friends, and *even our relatives over the holidays*. Aren't humble, vulnerable, and genuine people so nice to be around?

Think first about the foundations of humility. The higher your structure is to be, the deeper must be its foundation.

—St. Augustine

November 21

Happy Holidays?

We all know that there are many sad people during the holidays. Some are sad because they won't be with relatives; some are sad *because they will be.* (For proof of this, just look at all the sad and stressed-out people in the airports!) I've always said that most of us have at least one relative whom we can't handle without alcohol.

Seriously, though, whatever your situation is this season, it can be your best holiday season ever. No joke. It only depends on *you.* If you are a *"thanker"* and a *giver* in every situation, you will have a remarkable holiday.

PS. If you play the martyr when you give, it doesn't count.

November 22

Choose Sides Now

The Two Sides of the "A" Club
Anxiety vs. Awareness
Anger vs. Appreciation
Arrogance vs. Availability

Just in case you anticipate a challenge or two over the holidays:

- Be *aware* of the innate value of everyone you will be around.
- Be *appreciative* of all the good things you often take for granted.
- Be *available* to make a difference where you can.

Or, stay on the *other side,* with anxiety, anger, and arrogance—the potential mood changers and energy sappers that often accompany the holidays.

Your friends and relatives will be grateful.

Well—some of them might say, "What got into him?"

But do it anyway.

November 23

Drama-Free Holiday Tip

Feelers: Fear-Trigger: Conflict

Talkers: Fear-Trigger: Rejection

} People Focused

Doers: Fear-Trigger: Manipulation

Thinkers: Fear-Trigger: Inaccuracy

} Task Focused

So many misunderstandings with family members, friends, coworkers, and strangers occur because we expect people to respond as we would respond. We think that everyone feels and thinks (or should feel and think) as we do. If we utilized the information above concerning personality differences and considered the *fear-triggers* of different personality types before we tried to befriend, direct, praise, or correct, our successful response rate at the dinner table would skyrocket.*

This is usually much better for relationships than rolling our eyes, getting angry, or assuming people are bossy, boring, self-absorbed, selfish, or emotional.

By the way, people-focused feelers and talkers generally have more difficulty understanding task-focused doers and thinkers.

*If you are unsure of someone's type, just wait for his or her dominant style to surface.

November 24

Look! I Can Bend My Knee

While I was volunteering at Scottish Rite Hospital for Children as a receptionist, a five-year-old girl came to my desk to sign in for her appointment. With a joyfully expressive face and voice, she said, "Look! I can bend my knee!"

Her mother came behind her, explaining, "This is the first time since she was born that she has been able to do that without pain."

This memory came rushing to me just in time yesterday, while I was going through the motions of my life. My face lit up when I suddenly noticed that I could bend my knee—and my back without pain. I could smell popcorn and coffee. I could hear music. I could see where I was going. I could eat dinner. Wow!

A Clue to You

My friend Jan and I labored for years in restaurant management, while our creative gifts lay dormant; we were always complaining about our mediocre lives. When we read something profound, saw a creative, insightful new movie, or visited a new artist's gallery, we would frequently look at each other and say, "I could have done that." Secretly, we both resented the success of the innocent artisan.

(Not so) hidden message in our behavior: *you are ignoring your gift and calling.*

Jealousy, envy, discontent, excuses, blaming others, ache, longing, abject fear that *this is my life, this is all there is*—all translate to the same urgent message: get busy living and get busy changing!

November 26

Waking-Up's Message

Sleep is such a profound reminder of the utter dependence we have on a benevolent universe to sustain our lives. Have you ever meditated on the sheer absurdity of going comatose for several hours *every day?* This one reality should keep us completely aware of our humble dependence on a benevolent Creator.

Yet, on the other hand, if you woke up today, you can be sure of this: you have been given the power to make a difference in this world. You can be *absolutely* sure that someone needs you today.

God does not waste human resources.

Not Me?

I hate to admit this, but when my sister Angela was dying of cancer, we had an argument regarding the extent of support she required of me. I was resentful because she seemed not to take my personal and professional obligations into consideration. Ironically, my niece reminded me of this painful conversation when I was on my way to present a motivational address for caregivers. Until she brought it up, I had never fully grasped how wrong I had been.

What was I thinking? Certainly, I had a point—but being right was not as important as loving my sister in the last days of her life.

Dr. Henry Nouwen said, "It's easier to *be God* than to *love God in others*."

What a Nightmare!

I had a nightmare last night. I was dependent on someone else to validate my worth. The other person was not cooperating. I was desperate. The other person thought I was crazy and moved even farther away from me (primal scream!).

I woke up. Relief. I never have to be dependent on someone to validate my worth again. I am worthy. I am valuable. Just as I am. Let the smiles and the freedom begin.

Today, I move and act with confidence, aware of my unique voice, purpose, and value in this world. The world belongs to me. No one has to tell me that it does.

November 29

Mystery of the Deaf Dog, Solved

Our cocker spaniel, Chester, had just been groomed. Two little girls, probably four or five years old, came running behind him in the store, attempting to pet him. I said, "Chester really loves children, but he is deaf. He doesn't know you are here."

The girls stopped dead in their tracks, and the first one turned and signed to the other. The beautiful little girl broke out into a big smile of surprise and signed to me that she was deaf too. She sat down beside Chester, and they had a tearful "reunion."

All things have a purpose. Someone needs you today.

November 30

Control the Quality of Your Life

The quality of my life *today* is directly tied to how I think about life today. I can take charge of my happiness or choose to be a victim. If I choose to be a victim, if I choose to be negative, or if I choose to focus on fear and disappointment, life will continue to bring all these things. If I choose to be positive, confident, joyful, and generous, life will *always* bring me more of these things.

Do you ever wonder why you are not attracting the right people into your life?

Listen to your words.

Listen to your thoughts.

December

The Power of You

Because the people who are crazy enough to think they can change the world are the ones who do.

—*Steve Jobs*

December 1

Ouch, Ouch, Ouch!

Character is power.

—*Booker T. Washington*

On the days when I have been beaten down by circumstances or by someone else's malice or carelessness, it sure helps me to remember that many of my heroes have been imprisoned, abused, or worse.

In Nelson Mandela's *Long Road to Freedom*, he attests to the truth of Booker T. Washington's quote and honors his twenty-seven(!) years of imprisonment as the needed crucible of his character.

I'm not saying that we should be happy about pain and abuse. I'm just saying that the character we develop in difficulties will often prove to be worth the inconvenience.

There is a purity in pain that a noble heart will embrace
and honor
and treat as friend not foe.

December 2

Courage Is a Key

My mind frequently pulls up a scene at the beginning of *Dances with Wolves*, where the battalion is paralyzed with fear, but Kevin Costner's character breaks the battle stalemate by jumping onto his horse and riding boldly into the face of danger.

This scene reminds me of the importance of bravery in my own life. I don't have to wait for someone else to lead or someone else to take care of me. I don't have to spend my life complaining about the lack of leadership in the world. I can be, today, what the world needs.

We all admire someone who has courage. We are all looking for leaders who are fearless.

Brave people give us hope.

This is the day! *You were born to be bold!*

December 3

Take the Risk

Striking up a conversation with a stranger is difficult, especially when people keep to themselves or seem busy. While dragging in the last mile of a race event, I had to get my mind off myself, so I asked two teenagers (who had just started walking) to tell me about the cause that was advertised on their running shirts.

Their faces lit up, and the ensuing conversation was informative and energizing. It got all three of us running again, and we met several other interesting people as a result.

The other runners who were formerly just props in our world suddenly were animated, lovable, and interesting.

We all have so much in common, but we may never know it until someone risks one little question.

December 4

Fearlessly Affirm Your Gifts

I was at a networking meeting after I had just started my consulting business, when a dentist asked me, "Do you think you can help my employees?"

I answered, "I can sure try."

Needless to say, I didn't get the job.

Last week, I got a job inquiry from another country, but I didn't hear back for several days. I was afraid I was going to lose the account but stopped my angst by saying, "I know I can help these people. And I am confident that they will call me back if I am meant to make a difference for them!"

They called the next day and booked me.

What a difference affirmations have made for me!

Our *gifts* are for the world. We can use them with fearless confidence.

December 5

Sing Some Magic

In a recent seminar, a woman said that her daughter, whom she had just left at her first day of kindergarten, was terrified *until* another little girl took her hand and said, "Don't be afraid. This is a very good place. We're gonna sing songs."

The little girl's insight reminded me of the transformational power of music in all of our lives. The most mundane or demanding experience is transformed with the right song.

I've also concluded that *anyone's* life is more interesting to us if, behind their life, we add a proper musical score (and maybe a bag of popcorn).

December 6

Charge!

He only earns his freedom and his life who takes them every day by
storm.

—*Goethe*

A recurring theme in Goethe's writing is this relentlessness—

What you can do or think you can do; begin it.
For boldness has magic, power, and genius in it.

Or—

I love the person who yearns for the impossible.

Whatever your situation today, even if you are flat on your back,
keep taking your day by storm! You have nothing to lose—except
lethargy, discouragement, etc.

And, while you might have some failures, in them will be the
seeds of an even greater success.

And, by the way, your dreams are no less valuable than the dreams
of those who have already found success!

December 7

There's Lots of Room at the Top for *You*

I am not afraid of an army of lions led by a sheep; I am afraid of an army of sheep led by a lion.

—*Alexander the Great*

Alexander knew (from personal experience) the power of one. He knew that one strong person with courage and tenacity was a force that could turn a vulnerable multitude. He also knew there was a deficit of people who were willing to be this *one.*

One person (you) can make a big difference. It only takes one (you). The world desperately needs leaders (you).

In order to be a leader, we (you) simply must resist the temptation to complain, despair, or fret—*today*—and, instead, be the leader the world is waiting for.

December 8

Extra Rooms in Your House

Comedian Jane Wagner pokes: "A sobering thought: What if, at this very moment, I am living up to my full potential?"

Scary!

Of course, we've all heard about our unused potential. Yesterday, I remembered a recurring dream about finding many extra rooms in my house that I didn't know I had. I would be thinking, *why haven't I been using these?* They would have really come in handy.

Dream experts say that a house is a metaphor of our life.

I now know that I have always had lots of "extra, unused rooms in my house," and no one was keeping me from discovering and using them—except myself.

And *nothing* compares to the satisfaction of finally doing so!

December 9

Step off the Roller Coaster

Paying attention to my thoughts, I notice a roller-coaster trend: I move from up to down, light to dark, optimism to pessimism, confidence to worry, and hope to fear in a matter of moments.

Today, I corral the unpredictable nature of my thought life by listening to CDs about courageous people who made a difference *in spite of roller-coaster circumstances.*

As I listen, I notice that all of these role models were voracious readers, who realized (as I often forget) that all of us need help staying steady, strong, and hopeful.

Today, if you are riding the roller coaster, step off and go to "school" instead. *Read. Google* inspiring people. *Listen* to an audio. *Watch* your heroes on YouTube or TED.com. Get the support you need to make your path a steady climb upward.

December 10

What Are You Passionate About?

When someone inspires me, it is usually because of their passion. When someone accomplishes something significant, it is usually because of their passion. When I am attracted to someone, it is usually because of their passion. When the world changes, it is usually because of someone's passion.

Instead of asking what someone does for a living, what they are doing for the holidays, or how many children they have, I now ask, "What are you passionate about?" The answer (or lack of answer) to that question tells me more about a person than many other questions could.

What are you passionate about today?

December 11

Keep Pushing!

Effort only fully releases its reward after a person refuses to quit.

- Napoleon Hill

I don't know how it works, but this is always true.

Look for these "road signs." When you see them, you know your reward is waiting to be released to you, just around the corner:

- You feel like you can't go on.
- You feel like everything and everyone is against you.
- You feel like your life is meaningless.
- You have no energy remaining.
- You are broke or tragically in debt and don't know where your next meal will come from.
- You feel like a total failure.
- You feel like you have nothing to give to the people who need you.
- It will take a miracle to proceed.

Keep pushing. You are so close that Angels are holding their breath.

December 12

Power to Spare

Hey!

Today, please don't underestimate your power to overcome all the challenges of your life.

- You were created to be a contender and a champion!
- You don't have to live vicariously through the lives of celebrities or sports heroes.
- You are programmed to be a victor.
- You are up for the task.
- You are an inspiration and your story will be a legend.
- Women, men, and angels are watching you and cheering you to victory!
- You can live the big *Life* you have imagined.
- Your life matters more than you ever dreamed.
- Don't settle for the small life of defeat.
- Never give up.
- You have power to spare.

December 13

Certificate of Attendance?

I don't want a *Certificate of Attendance* for showing up today.

I want the first place ribbon. I run the race as if to win.

Making it through another day or merely churning it out isn't going to cut it.

So, I'm going to turn on the joy. I'm going to *immerse* myself in this day. I'm going to *feel* it, *experience* all of it—even if I am sitting in a dental chair, getting five root canals done.

Because I know that, today, many are getting chemo, watching loved ones die, or struggling to recover after tragedy.

And I know that my life *can* make a difference, add value, and give hope if I am completely *aware, appreciative,* and *available* to *all* this day brings.

Because people are counting on me—I'm going to win.

December 14

Emerson's Challenge to Me

All I have seen teaches me to trust the Creator for all I have not seen.

—*Ralph Waldo Emerson*

Yep. The same guy who said *that* also caused a major ruckus in the church over his *self-reliance* doctrine. It makes complete sense to me—*now*.

For many years, I thought ideas of self-sufficiency and relying on God were mutually exclusive. This is how I have recently reconciled them: The Creator created us with the power to choose our destiny and to play, love, and laugh along the way. Fully utilizing the depth of this mystery is the essence of relying on God and the majesty that has been freely given to all.

Self-sufficiency is complete trust and awareness of *God within*.

December 15

Neuroplasticity to the Rescue

The Brain That Changes Itself, by Dr. Norman Doidge, is about the ability our brains have to create new pathways for our physiological and psychological functions.

Brain neuroplasticity offers a message of *hope* because it is more evidence that we never have to be held captive by our circumstances. I believe that many times, the first step into mental illness is feeling like we have no options. When, we, as humans, feel trapped or hopeless, we exhibit harmful behaviors.

If you haven't yet, watch Christopher de Charms, Charles Limb, Jill Bolte Taylor, and other scientists on *TED.com,* and be encouraged!

Important neuroplasticity fact: thoughts produce deep channels in your brain. You can change your brain by changing your thoughts. Wow!

December 16

No Life Is Wasted Who Has Lightened the Load of Another

Charles Dickens wrote this in his book, *Our Mutual Friend,* about a cleaning woman who rescued an orphan. She lived and died in obscurity but made an immeasurable difference through the life she saved.

Sometimes, I forget that we were born to "lighten loads," that nothing about us is a mistake, and that our peculiarities, circumstances, and passions are part of a really big mysterious puzzle.

We never really know the difference we are making or the ripple effect of our lives. By being *who we are* and accepting ourselves *with love and joy,* we will make a difference for someone who desperately needs help with their load today.

December 17

Emotional Dominance!

Justifying their moodiness, I constantly hear this excuse from "mature" adults: "I'm always in a good mood—unless something bad happens or someone does something stupid."

No wonder the world is so full of unpredictable volatility and depression! Unfortunately, the only thing that *is* predictable is that people *will* do stupid stuff (including you) and that *(seemingly)* bad things *will* happen.

The *only* cure for this madness is emotional dominance. And the only way you get emotional dominance is by tuning-up your state of mind *every day*. If you expect a good day, you will have to be ready for everything*!*

The state of your life is nothing more than a reflection of your state of mind.

—*Wayne Dyer*

December 18

The Adjustment Bureau

I watched a movie recently called *The Adjustment Bureau* and was inspired to challenge fate. I was challenged to push harder for the things I believe in. I was challenged not to give up or think something is of no use.

Even though the movie was simplistic and the premise was extreme, the message was one of importance: our personal power to make things different is much greater than we have ever imagined.

Today, I hope you will fight for what you believe in. I hope you will see how your life makes a difference. I hope you will resist the temptation to give up.

The world desperately needs people like this. Your character, courage, and tenacity are critical.

Each one of us *can* be the leader the world is waiting for.

December 19

Meet Amazing People Every Week

I am *amazed* at all the amazing people I meet in a week. They are everywhere! I cannot go anywhere without meeting someone who wows me.

About this, my pessimistic friends say, "That's because they are all *single-serving friends*. You don't know them well enough. That's why you think they are amazing," or, "I never meet interesting people. It's probably because you travel."

But my optimistic friends say, "I know! Me too!"

Wanted: Heroes

Abraham Lincoln appointed Grant as field commander during the Civil War after five previous commanders had failed to take definitive action and help him bring an end to the carnage. Grant led courageously on the battlefield by acting *as if he were already dead*.

His passionate approach was not popular with the other officers. One of them reported to Lincoln that Grant had been drinking while on duty. Lincoln replied insightfully to the messenger, "Find out what he is drinking, and send it to all the other officers."

Lincoln knew that Grant's weaknesses were minor compared with the impact his life was having upon the world. It's a very rare individual, indeed, who seizes opportunities with Grant's brand of commitment.

December 21

Living Like I'm Already Dead

My kids accuse me of having a death wish, but it's not that I want to die, just that I'm not afraid of dying. I used to be the biggest chicken in the whole world: totally paranoid about pain, death, and the unknown. Two things changed me.

1. I survived a near-death experience and felt a mysterious spiritual support during the ordeal.
2. I observed the abject freedom that people enjoy when (like General Grant) they live *as if they are already dead* or have nothing else to lose.

We all have to die. We might as well make it count for something. One person's courage can make a difference for many.

December 22

We Are All Catalytic Converters

Last night I dreamed of *catalytic converters*. Really. When I looked up what they were this morning, I realized the importance and the connection in my dream.

I was dreaming about the importance of positive energy and how to convert bad energy into good energy to improve my state of mind and the states of mind of those around me.

A catalytic converter stimulates a chemical reaction in which toxic byproducts of combustion are converted to less toxic substances.

The catalyst is *what I think about.*

My thoughts produce chemical reactions that convert the toxic byproducts of *self-combustion.*

What a difference we can make—today!

December 23

Go Live the Life of Your Dreams

I couldn't wait for success, so I went ahead without it.

—*Jonathan Winters*

I remember how frightened I was, venturing out to use my creative and motivational gifts. I remember how guilty I felt using all my savings to do so. I remember the first time I told someone I was a speaker—I felt like I was exaggerating.

I remember feeling *honored* when I received my first *honorarium* (even though it was only fifty dollars).

I remember feeling giddy holding my first check for acting in my hands.

I remember the disbelief when I finished writing my first full-length screenplay.

And I remember the horrible feeling of believing that *I would never be able to do what I loved for a living.*

December 24

Never Without Purpose

Three years ago, I was feeling anonymous and inconsequential, on a cold and rainy day, walking among the masses on the sidewalks of downtown Auckland.

Then, Neil, a salon owner from Cambodia, talked to me while he was cutting my hair. When I was leaving, he gave me a valuable gift by saying, "You made my day. You are the friendliest person I have ever met!"

His words meant so much that I recorded them in my journal. I'm glad I did. I was back in New Zealand last week, so I looked up his shop, and we encouraged each other again.

Neil and I agree on two things:

1. the importance of making someone's day
2. every day and every person has a purpose

December 25

When Evidence Isn't Evident

Several Christmases back, I went into a black hole of depression because I couldn't see any tangible evidence that my life had really made a difference. While stuck in a traffic jam, tired and discouraged, I said out loud, "What does it matter if I'm a good person? Who really cares, anyway?"

My preteen niece and daughters, who were in the backseat of the car, suddenly got quiet. My niece Susannah said, *"It matters to us!"*

Stuck in traffic yesterday on the Lincoln Memorial Circle, I thought about how Lincoln persevered, even though the Civil War was so disheartening to him. I'm glad he took the long view. *It mattered to me.*

Happy holiday—*regardless of the evidence!*

December 26

The You Inside Wants Out

Ten years ago (and this had never happened to me before), I felt an urge to paint a picture. My hands literally were aching, as if something wanted *to come out of my fingers.*

I found something to paint on and opened all the leftover cans of house paint in the garage and started my first picture. I now have painted a whole houseful of abstracts and landscapes.

I persuaded my friend Jan to take a painting class with me, and she told me she was not creative and had no artistic ability. She was the star student in the class and now shows and sells her art.

I'll never buy that line from *anyone* again.

December 27

No Comparison

It occurs to me that when I feel the most discouraged about *me* is when I compare my gifts, my abilities, my future possibilities, or my options with those of someone else. Doing that, I always come to the conclusion that I have nothing new to offer and that my life is in no way unique or noteworthy.

So, in this moment, I acknowledge that there is *no comparison*.

I am here, in this place, at this time, with these longings for a *specific purpose*. The impulses and gifts I have are electromagnetic energy urging me toward a place *I must go* (for the sake of who-knows-who) into the unfathomable manifestation of my mysterious and magnificent life.

December 28

Just Today

People think that at the top there isn't much room. They tend to think of it as an Everest. My message is that there is tons of room at the top.

—*Margaret Thatcher*

She would know, having come from obscurity to be one of the most respected prime ministers of Great Britain.

And because there is so much room at the top, for the sake of the good we can do,

- *We must live our best lives today;*
- We must resist the temptation to be fearful;
- We must resist the temptation to be negative; and
- We must resist the temptation to be little.

So many people are counting on us. We were born to make a difference.

Please do so—today—*just today.*

Tomorrow will take care of itself.

Nothing is Wasted

My friend Catherine told me her husband's story:

"Ted sat outside his apartment, holding a complete stranger who had just shot himself. As the life was seeping out of the middle-aged man, Ted desperately prayed that this stranger would survive until help arrived. *No miracle occurred.*"

But there is a longer story.

What the dead man's family doesn't know is that Ted's life was forever changed that day. As the life was leaving the man he was holding, Ted latched on to life with a new commitment to live with his whole heart. Ted had also been depressed and defeated. Now, Ted's life is bringing hope to others—*because of the stranger's suicide.*

Tragedy. Sadness. But there is a longer story.

Nothing is wasted.

December 30

Never, Never Give Up

Always continue the climb.
It is possible for you to do whatever you choose,
if you first get to know who you are and
are willing to work with a power that is greater than yourself to do it.

—*Ella Wheeler Wilcox*

At forty-five, I thought my life was over, that I had missed my calling, and that I was doomed to a mediocre purgatory. In reality, I was approaching the beginning of a most remarkable life.

The days of saying, "I can't," and "You just don't understand," and "Poor me," are so far gone that the memories now seem to be from someone else's life.

As long as there is life, there is hope.

Never give up.

December 31

Stop! Dig Deep Before You Proceed

You have what it takes! Today, right now—before you launch into what you want the new year to be, or how the new year has to be different from the old year, or what the new year has to be in order for you to be happy—*simply be happy!*

Just stop. Feel your breath. Be aware of the miracle of you: *you, alive right now, in this moment.*

This thoughtful moment has the power to bring you into a simple state of acceptance and awareness, which always leads to gratitude. And gratitude *always* leads to happiness. And isn't that what you want in the new year?

Let us not look back in anger or forward in fear,
but around in awareness.

—*James Thurber*

Bibliography

Allen, David. *Getting Things Done: The Art of Stress-Free Productivity.* Viking Penguin, 2001.

Angelou, Maya. *I Know Why the Caged Bird Sings.* Random House, 1969.

Baer, Ulrich. *The Wisdom of Rilke.* Random House, 2005.

Bethge, Eberhard. *Bonhoeffer.* HarperCollins, 1979.

Bok, Edward. *The Americanization of Edward Bok.* Scribner, 1920.

Braybrooke, Marcus. *Bridge of Stars.* Duncan Baird Publishers, 2001.

Brown, Brené. *The Gifts of Imperfection.* Hazelden, 2010.

Carnegie, Andrew. *The Autobiography of Andrew Carnegie.* Signet Classics, 2006.

Chopra, Deepak. *The Seven Spiritual Laws of Success.* Amber–Allen Publishing, 1993.

————. *Magical Mind, Magical Body.* Nightingale Conant, 2000.

Chu, Chin-Ning. *Thick Face, Black Heart.* AMC Publishing, 1992.

Coelho, Paulo. *The Alchemist.* HarperCollins, 1993.

Day, Dorothy. *The Long Loneliness.* Harper & Row, 1952.

Dickens, Charles. *Our Mutual Friend*. Modern Library, 2002.

_____. *A Tale of Two Cities*. Penguin Classics, 2003.

Dickenson, Emily. *Selected Poems of Emily Dickinson*. Random House. 1924.

Doidge, Norman. *The Brain that Changes Itself.* Viking Penguin, 2007.

Dooley, Mike. *Notes from the Universe*. Atria Books, 2003.

_____. *Infinite Possibilities*. Atria Books, 2009.

Follett, Ken. *Pillars of the Earth*. New American Library, 1990.

Frankl, Victor. *Man's Search for Meaning*. Beacon Press, 1959.

Franklin, Benjamin. *The Autobiography of Ben Franklin*. Oxford University Press, 2009.

Gaarder, Jostein. *Sophie's World*. Farrar, Straus and Giroux, 1994

Gibran, Kahlil. *The Prophet*. Alfred A. Knopf, 1923.

Giovanni, Janine di. *Madness Visible, A Memoir of War*. Bloomsbury, 2004.

Grandin, Temple. *The Way I See It*. Future Horizons, 2011.

Hillesum, Etty. *An Interrupted Life*. Random House, 1986.

Hosseini, Khaled. *A Thousand Splendid Suns*. Riverhead Books, 2007.

_____. *The Kite Runner*. Riverhead Books, 2003.

Lansing, Alfred. *Endurance, Shackleton's Incredible Voyage*. Carroll & Graf, 1986.

Maltz, Maxwell. *Psycho-Cybernetics*. Prentice-Hall, 1960.

Muggeridge, Malcolm. *Something Beautiful for God*. Harper & Row, 1971.

Nouwen, Henri. *The Wounded Healer: Ministry in Contemporary Society*. Doubleday, 1979.

————. *Gracias! A Latin American Journal*. Orbis Books, 1983.

Ponder, Catherine. *The Dynamic Laws of Prosperity*. BN Publishing, 2008.

Rand, Ayn. *Atlas Shrugged*. Plume, 1999.

Richie, George. *Return from Tomorrow,* Chosen Books, 2007.

Robinson, John Elder. *Be Different*. Crown Archetype, 2011.

————. *Look Me in the Eye*. Crown Publishers, 2007.

Sebold, Alice. *The Lovely Bones*. Little, Brown and Company, 2002.

Shinn, Florence Scovel. *The Game of Life and How to Play It*. Prosperity Classic, 1925.

————. *Your Word is Your Wand*. Zulu Books, 2011.

Silverstein, Shel. *Where the Sidewalk Ends*. Harper & Row, 1974.

Stevenson, Robert Louis. *Aes Triplex*. Nabu Press, 2011.

Tammet, Daniel. *Born on a Blue Day,* Free Press, 2006.

Ten Boom, Corrie. *The Hiding Place*. Chosen Books, 1971.

Tolle, Eckhart. *A New Earth*. Penguin Group, 2005

Whitman, Walt. *Leaves of Grass*. Quality Paperback Book Club, 1992.

Wilcox, Ella Wheeler. *The Best of Ella Wheeler Wilcox*. 2007.

Williamson, Marianne. *Return to Love*. HarperCollins, 1992.

Vujicic, Nick. *Life Without Limits*. Doubleday, 2010.

Zander, Rosamund Stone and Benjamin. *The Art of Possibility*. Harvard Business School Press, 2000.

Ziglar, Zig. *Over the Top*. Thomas Nelson, 1997.